Your Grown-Up Faith

Blending the Three Elements of Belief

KENNETH L. PARKER

INSPIRED BY THE SPIRITUAL LIFE OF BLESSED JOHN HENRY CARDINAL NEWMAN

Liguori
LIGUORI, MISSOURI

Imprimi Potest:
Harry Grile, CSsR, Provincial
Denver Province, The Redemptorists

Published by Liguori Publications
Liguori, Missouri 63057

To order, call 800-325-9521
www.liguori.org

Library of Congress Cataloging-in-Publication Data

Parker, Kenneth L.
Your grown-up faith: blending the three elements of belief/Kenneth L. Parker.—1st ed.
p. cm.
"Inspired by the spiritual life of Blessed John Henry Cardinal Newman."
1. Spiritual life—Catholic Church. 2. Faith development. 3. Newman, John Henry, 1801-1890. I. Newman, John Henry, 1801-1890. II. Title.
BX2178.P37 2012
248.4'82—dc23
2012030275

p ISBN 978-0-7648-2221-6
e ISBN 978-0-7648-6738-5

Liguori Publications, a nonprofit corporation, is an apostolate of The Redemptorists. To learn more about The Redemptorists, visit Redemptorists.com.

Printed in the United States of America
16 15 14 13 12 / 5 4 3 2 1
First Edition

Dedicated to my three sons,
Geoffrey, Emanuel, and Luke

Contents

Preface

A project like this is never completed without the help and guidance of many mentors, friends, and loved ones. I am deeply grateful to Professor Lawrence Barmann, who has taught me so much about Baron Friedrich von Hügel, and his concept of the three elements of religion. This book is the fruit of hundreds of conversations and sessions with students, parishioners, and friends over the last twenty years. They have helped me understand the three elements of belief and sharpened my appreciation for this way of analyzing a believer's faith journey. The monks and oblates of Ascension Monastery in Jerome, Idaho, heard early versions of these chapters during a retreat in May 2011. Their enthusiasm convinced me to complete this project.

Luis Medina of Liguori Publications has been a consistent source of support and encouragement during the process of preparing this book. In the final stages of editing the text, students in the spring 2012 creative writing class at the Eastern Region Diagnostic and Corrections Center gave this book a serious read and close critique. Within that class, I am particularly indebted to Mr. Cory Gardner and Mr. Raymond Scott, who are the best copyeditors I have ever had! Thanks must also be extended to doctoral students at Saint Louis University, who took time out of a busy semester to offer advice and make recommendations. They helped me adjust theological nuances and clarify points of history and doctrine.

Finally, I thank my three sons, Geoffrey, Emanuel, and Luke, who remain a constant inspiration and source of joy. No father has ever been more blessed. I marvel at their kindness, generosity of spirit, and patience. Their contagious sense of humor keeps me laughing and helps me remember not to take myself too seriously. This book is dedicated to them in the hopes that they will remain true to their journey of faith, and learn in God's timing how to blend the three elements of belief.

SAINT LOUIS, MISSOURI
FEAST OF SAINT ATHANASIUS
MAY 2, 2012

You picked up this book because you want a "grown-up" faith. This is a natural human desire. John Henry Newman rightly observed, "we must believe something." The real question is not if you believe, but what you believe. In the early twenty-first century, the great temptation is to let the immediacy of non-stop media and the pressures of everyday life crowd out those things that draw you into the presence of God and mature your spiritual life. Yet if your Christian faith does not mold who you are, the world will. Saint Paul said it best: "Do not be conformed to this world, but be transformed by the renewing of your minds, so that you may discern what is the will of God—what is good and acceptable and perfect." (Romans 12:2)

But how do you make progress on your journey of faith? This book is designed to help you do just that. Like you, I struggled for years to understand what it means to be a person of faith. The longing was there, but I was conscious of different parts of me pulling in what seemed contradictory directions. They appeared to be in conflict. Is faith about believing what I have been taught by authorities in my life—by parents, teachers, priests, bishops, and the pope? Or should I be skeptical about everything that authorities have told me is true and seek out proofs that will satisfy my mind? Maybe faith is not about dogmas and rules at all and is more about listening to the "inner voice" that guides me through my unique life experiences—being spiritual but not religious. If you have puzzled over any of these aspects of your faith, then this book is intended for you.

Everyone's life experience is different, so you are probably wondering if I have anything useful to share. In this book I will tell you a bit about my story of faith and explain what I have learned about the common themes discovered in the lives of others. I particularly want to draw on the life and writings of Blessed John Henry Cardinal Newman, whose remarkable life of faith is a rich resource for all of us. Although he lived in the 1800s, Newman's Christian life provides a moving example of the blessings and challenges that come from being a Christian in the fullest possible sense. Emerging from all of this is something that I call the three elements of belief.

The Three Elements of Belief

> Listen, O my son, to the precepts of thy master, and incline the ear of thy heart, and cheerfully receive and faithfully execute the admonitions of a loving Father, that by the toil of obedience thou mayest return to Him from whom by the sloth of disobedience thou has gone away. To thee, therefore, my speech is now directed, who, giving up thine own will, takest up the strong and most excellent arms of obedience to do battle for Christ the Lord, the true King.
>
> PROLOGUE, RULE OF SAINT BENEDICT

In the spring of 1977 I heard these words for the first time while visiting Saint Andrew's Abbey, a Benedictine monastery in the Mojave Desert of California. They pierced my heart and called me toward a new path in life. Though a Southerner who had only recently arrived in the Los Angeles basin—Hollywood, drugs, and sex had not lured me westward. I was a twenty-two-year-old Protestant seminarian studying at Fuller Theological Seminary in Pasadena, California. On Sundays, I often attended two or three different church services and spent my leisure hours in informal theological debates rather than dancing at discotheques or improving my tan on the beach.

Nevertheless, I was living in rebellion. As the son of a successful Protestant pastor and profoundly devout evangelical mother, I had fled to the other side of the country to escape a father who—I imagined—wanted nothing more than to call me back from "the sloth of disobedience." On more than one occasion, in the midst of heated encounters over my life and faith, Mother admonished me to accept Dad's instructions. "Your father wants what is best for you," she would say. "It is better to obey than to seek your own will." I would not—could not—comply.

However, the path to which Benedict called me was not back to North Carolina and my earthly father, but toward an unthinkable future as a Roman Catholic—and even to consider the possibility of being a monk (a vocation I tested for five years after I became a Roman Catholic). Could this be the voice of God calling to me, though the words were written in the early sixth century? That question haunted me for the next six years as I struggled against the prospect of such a painful, life-altering step. Surely God did not expect such a sacrifice.

After finishing a master's degree in historical theology at Fuller Seminary, I continued my studies at the University of Cambridge and focused my research on English Reformation Studies. In part I sought reasons for remaining a Protestant and grounds for rejecting Roman Catholicism. Out of love for my parents I yearned to return to my evangelical roots and live out the Christian faith within the parameters of my received heritage. Yet there was no escaping the call I had heard in the desert.

In the summer of 1981, during a seven-day retreat at Quarr Abbey on the Isle of Wight in the south of England, my future became more clear. Father Joseph Warralow, the monastery's guestmaster and the only priest I knew in England, had devoted much of that week to exploring the reasons why I should not become a Catholic. I knew the history of the Church, its many failures, and the scandals of its structures and leaders. I had serious questions about doctrines and devotional practices that felt alien, incomprehensible, and even repulsive. Father Joseph warned me that becoming a Roman Catholic might sever me from the love of my parents and cause friends to shun me. Yet during an afternoon walk along the monastery's chestnut tree lane, I let go of fears about my future and set aside all the rational critiques I had amassed against the Roman Catholic Church. God was leading me down a path I did not know toward a spiritual home filled with unfamiliar customs and beliefs. I prayed for guidance and relaxed in the hope that clarity would follow.

I relate these events because they illustrate the theme of this book: the three elements of belief. During more than twenty years of teaching theology at Saint Louis University, I have been inspired by Friedrich von Hügel's book *The Mystical Element of Religion* and have taught my students what he called the "three elements of religion." This way of reflecting on religious experience is at once simple and profound. The three elements—the Child's Way, the Youth's Way, and the Adult's Way—are easily understood, for they are drawn from our lived experience. And use of this analogy will help you to recognize how all of these aspects of belief contribute to a "grown-up" faith.

John Henry Newman's life story is one of the best examples of how to blend these three elements of belief. He was formed in childhood to be a devout Protestant. In adolescence and early manhood, Newman struggled with questions about his faith; and after a long period of inner turmoil he slowly came to realize that he must become a Roman Catholic. His intentional Christian life gave him perceptive insights into the three elements of belief. As I have studied Newman's life and thought for over twenty years, in this book I use his experiences and writings—along with my own—to illustrate the three elements of belief.

The Child's Way—The First Element of Belief

My earliest memories are of the large Bible that sat on the coffee table in the living room, Dad's sing-song preaching voice (so typical of Southern ministers of that time), and Mother helping my older brother memorize Psalm 1 in his upper bunk bed while I lay quietly below, saying the words under my breath. My life began in a Southern state in the 1950s where fewer than one-half of one percent of the population was Roman Catholic. I knew that to be saved meant going to the front of church (what we called the mourner's bench), asking God to forgive my sins and being surrounded by adults who encouraged and prayed for me. From my grandmother I learned that the pope was the Antichrist and that mainline Protestants were merely Sunday Christians. I lived among the chosen few, who were called to live in sinless perfection and faultless obedience to all of God's laws. These experiences formed my childhood religious imagination.

The Child's Way of religious belief is largely shaped by authorities and the religious environment they create. My early understanding of belief came through people, places, and things. Authorities, institutions, religious objects, and customs shaped what I took to be the external "facts" about Christian faith. For me, these beliefs came from the denominational tradition I was raised in. It was authority-focused and marked by trusting obedience. These memories affect me to this day and remain a powerful context for my life as a believer.

The Youth's Way—The Second Element of Belief

With the onset of puberty and teenage years came new experiences of the world. My parents took me on trips abroad to the Middle East and Europe. And as my teenage years advanced I traveled in South America, Africa, and Asia. I witnessed Christian worship in other churches and met persons who practiced other religions. One of my best friends in junior high school was Jewish. Though I had opportunities to preach to tribal peoples in Surinam as a teenager and smuggled Bibles into the Soviet Union in my early twenties, the religious experiences of those I sought to evangelize deeply troubled me. The sincerity and devotion of those outside my church tradition defied the categories I had been taught.

I puzzled over the behavioral prohibitions of my church. I wanted to go to the junior high school socials...and dance! Yet even more disturbing to my parents, as a teenager I began to puzzle about the core teachings of our church. In my college and seminary years, so much that I learned cast doubt on church teachings received as a child. Could anyone really achieve sinless perfection? Why was it so easy to sin and fall from grace, only to repeat the cycle at the mourner's bench over and over again? When I sought explanations, my questions met with exasperation or worse. When the authorities of my childhood faith failed to answer my questions, I sought knowledge from other sources.

This inquisitive, testing aspect of faith, with its curiosity about religion's boundaries and possibilities is called the Youth's Way. This element of belief dominated my life from junior high school to doctoral studies at Cambridge University. Experiences outside home and the church community had stimulated an intense religious curiosity. There seemed to be contradictions between the "facts" of my childhood faith and the complexity of the world. While not consciously desiring to "rebel," I doubted the truth of certain doctrines and practices of my church. I wanted childhood authorities to take this impulse for rational discussion and debate seriously. When this trustful questioning met with fear, rebuke, and anger, I began to read books about Christianity and other religious traditions. I sought out people of faith who were not afraid of my questions. Religious experiences that stimulated new ways of thinking about and living out my faith were explored. This intellectual quest took directions that I did not intend or desire. After fifteen years of questioning and study, I reached a crossroad between the Child's Way that had formed my early religious imagination and the Youth's Way, which had grown out of a life of study and wide-ranging experiences.

In the Youth's Way, logical explanations for tenets of belief are demanded, and there is resistance to relying on authorities for answers where reason can be applied. It is an experience of faith that is rational, inquisitive, and marked by curiosity. For someone like me, this element of belief became a dominant aspect of my faith. It remains a strong dimension of my life as a believer and explains why I enjoy studying and teaching theology. This desire to understand is a compulsion.

The Adult's Way—The Third Element of Belief

In the afternoon sun of that summer day at Quarr Abbey, the inner conviction to become a Roman Catholic marked the emergence of the third element of belief in my life. The Adult's Way is the element of belief which is a step beyond the received religion of the Child's Way and the rationally analyzed belief systems of the Youth's Way. It is one that leads toward an experiential faith, that is not an external "fact" or a "system of ideas" to be analyzed, but a lived, internalized faith. Mental prayer, contemplative reading of sacred and revered texts, and the sacraments become aids to this inner growth of faith. These nourish the soul.

This third element has also been called the Ethico-Mystical Way because the conviction to act runs beyond what external authorities can impart and systems of belief can explain. It is a turning point, when faith becomes an interior, guiding principle. It defines who you are and motivates your choices. My growth into the Catholic Church was not intended or even desired but became a call to action that could not be resisted without serious harm to my Christian life. The Adult's Way has been the compass that has guided my spiritual journey down to the present.

In the Adult's Way, Christian belief is internalized, the

limits of human religious authorities are acknowledged, and the insufficiency of human reason is recognized. There is a profound need to discover through active commitment the full meaning of the deepest principles of belief. This experience causes a fundamental change, or conversion, in one's life. It is an experience of faith that is ethical, mystical, and marked by compassion and love for God and neighbor.

How to Use this Book

This book is intended to help you explore the meaning of the three elements of belief—the Child's Way, the Youth's Way, and the Adult's Way—in your life, and consider how these elements of belief, balanced in your life, can lead to greater insight into your experience of God, the Christian community that nurtures your faith, and the world which needs your example of living a "grown-up" faith.

Two chapters will be devoted to each of the three elements, and the concluding chapter will address how a healthy interaction of the three elements of belief can assist in the growth of even the most mature Christian. Like you, my own journey of faith continues to challenge and change me; but perhaps God can use this book to guide you toward deeper reflection on these matters. May Saint Benedict's closing words of the Prologue guide your thoughts as you read this book; for "as we advance in the...faith, we shall run the way of God's commandments with expanded hearts and unspeakable sweetness of love."

SECTION I

The First Element of Belief

CHAPTER ONE

Receiving a Religious Imagination

Truly I say to you, whoever does not receive the kingdom of God as a little child will never enter it.

LUKE 18:17

Christianity is not a matter of opinion, but an external fact, entering into, carried out in, indivisible from, the history of the world.

JOHN HENRY NEWMAN
CERTAIN DIFFICULTIES FELT BY ANGLICANS (1857), 290

The Church is a collection of souls, brought together
in one by God's secret grace,
though that grace comes to them through visible
instruments,
and unites them to a visible hierarchy.
What is seen is not the whole of the Church,
but the visible part of it.

JOHN HENRY NEWMAN
SERMONS PREACHED ON VARIOUS OCCASIONS, (1857), 65

John Henry Newman once observed, "children's minds are impressible in a very singular way, such as is not common afterwards." If you are like me, you look back on your childhood and probably remember only vignettes and have forgotten all the rest. In matters of faith, Newman concluded that these form the basis for your religious imagination, which is "traceable to a few external circumstances" (*Parochial and Plain Sermons*, 4:46, 1849). Often a single event or memory can shape crucial aspects of your Christian faith and how you practice your beliefs.

Newman's observations can be illustrated in the early childhood experiences of Saint Thérèse of Lisieux, who as a young girl grew up in a family and parish that instilled a rich religious imagination. The impact was so profound that she entered the Carmelite Convent in Lisieux, France, at age fifteen, and lived an exemplary life until her tragically young death at age twenty-four in 1897. Under obedience to her mother superior, she wrote an autobiography called *Story of a Soul*. One of her earliest memories was of blessed bread.

Until the rise of frequent communion in the Roman Catholic Church at the urging of Pope Pius X in 1905, the more common experience at Sunday Mass was receiving ordinary bread that had been blessed at the offertory (*pain bénit*). Nineteenth-century French Catholics commonly took blessed bread home to those unable to attend because of sickness or other impediments. For young children, this became their experience of "communion" in the years prior to receiving the Eucharist.

Thérèse of Lisieux described this practice as one of her first memories of religion. During her earliest years, Thérèse's mother stayed home with her rather than take her to Mass. Her slightly older sister Céline commonly returned with blessed bread for her little sister, though on occasion the supply at church ran out and she returned empty-handed. Thérèse remembered on at least one Sunday complaining that she could not go without her "Mass" and asking her sister to make blessed bread for her.

> *Céline immediately opened the cupboard, took out the bread, cut a tiny bit off, and after saying a Hail Mary quite solemnly over it, triumphantly presented it to me; and I, making the sign of the cross, ate it with devotion, fancying it tasted exactly like the real blessed bread.*

Clearly, Thérèse was a precociously religious child. Her mother reported in a letter to Thérèse's older sister, Marie, "Céline said the other day: 'How can God be in such a tiny host?' Thérèse answered: 'That is not strange, because God is Almighty!' 'And what does Almighty mean?' [Céline asked. Thérèse replied,] 'It means that He can do whatever He likes.'"

While it is tempting for some to read Thérèse's *Story of a Soul* with a cynical attitude because of its sweet, innocent tone, her earliest memories are examples of the Child's Way. The child gains her impressions of religion from what she sees and is told. It is a fact, a thing—the foundation on which her Christian belief is built.

The five senses play a dominant role in shaping the Child's Way. To the young child's senses, symbols and places, images and objects, ritualized gestures and postures all play a role in understanding the outward realities of religious practice. Through parents, older siblings, clergy, and teachers, an "authoritative" understanding of religion is cultivated. I use the word "authoritative" because this is knowledge mediated by trusted people, institutions, and traditional practices. It is rooted in the past, in custom, and communal patterns of belief and ritual that are an external reality.

For Thérèse, God's presence in the world—and God's capacity to be present in the Eucharist—were self-evident realities. The authority she granted her slightly older sibling, to bless bread in the absence of bread blessed by a priest, illustrates the trust a child often places in those who help shape his or her religious imagination.[1]

I recall being struck by the power of these childhood experiences during a conversation with a prominent Roman Catholic scholar at Cambridge University. As I prepared to become a Catholic during 1981 and 1982, this theologian took

1 Friedrich von Hügel, *The Mystical Element of Religion: As Studied in Saint Catherine of Genoa and Her Friends* (New York: E.P. Dutton and Co., 1923), 51.

an interest and often asked about my catechetical instruction. On one occasion I admitted that I still struggled with theological questions typical for anyone raised a Protestant. When pressed, I admitted that chief among these difficulties was the doctrine of transubstantiation. This Roman Catholic theologian expressed great surprise at this and admitted that he found my struggle incomprehensible. I insisted that he explain. Because this man was a prominent scholar, I expected a densely theological explanation of the intellectual developments that had resulted in the doctrine of transubstantiation. I anticipated hearing about how medieval theologians, in an effort to explain this mystery, borrowed Aristotle's distinction between an object's "substance" (what something is at its core) and "accident" (what we experience through our senses), to explain why the "substance" of consecrated bread was "trans"-formed into the body of Christ while continuing to appear to be bread. I expected him to remind me that the term was used at the Fourth Lateran Council in 1215 and formally defined by the Council of Trent in 1551, and that this should be accepted because councils have historically settled doctrinal questions.

Instead, he paused and told me about growing up as a Roman Catholic in the 1950s. He remembered that at age seven he had been given a rosary and wanted to have it blessed. Somehow he had gotten it into his head that the way to do this was to touch it with the blessed sacrament—the consecrated bread of the Eucharist. So the next Sunday after receiving communion he held the host on his tongue rather than swallow it, returned to his pew, pulled out his new rosary, and put it to his tongue.

At this point he became very animated and relived the horror of discovering that the host had become mangled in the chain and beads. He saw Christ's body mixed with his saliva and exposed to the indignity of his actions. As if living in that moment again he described the anxiety that filled him and fear of divine judgment for such a sacrilegious act. Then he broke away suddenly and said in his usual calm and measured way, "I don't understand why you struggle with the Real Presence of Christ in the Eucharist."

Like Thérèse of Lisieux, my Cambridge mentor found in those earliest memories of religion a powerful foundation that had shaped his religious imagination and sense of God's presence in the world. Education and adult experiences of faith had not diminished the importance of those memories as foundations for his later religious convictions.

Yet it is possible engage the Child's Way in circumstances other than experiences of biological childhood. I recall very well my earliest period of monastic formation in 1986, after finishing my doctorate at Cambridge, and the necessary "regression" into a childlike state during my novitiate. Following the direction of Benedict's Rule, I willingly submitted my will to the instruction of my religious superiors. Having been raised as an evangelical Protestant, a reshaped religious imagination was my goal. This meant accepting the words of those who instructed me and living out the truths imparted to me by trusted authorities.

One of the most vivid memories centered on living in deep reverence for Christ's presence in the Eucharist. This had not been part of my childhood religious imagination. The experience of being a sacristan (person who prepares a church for Mass) brought me into direct contact with this mystery and filled me with growing awe—and on at least one occasion, paralyzing dread.

During our annual fall festival at Saint Andrew's Abbey, I maintained order in the chapel as our priests held nonstop Masses throughout the weekend celebration. Because of the large crowds, our priests had, in previous weeks, consecrated thousands of hosts to ensure a sufficient supply in the ciborium (a container used to store consecrated hosts). My responsibilities included helping the priest distribute Communion to the people. Halfway through the weekend, as I held the ciborium and distributed the hosts to people attending Mass, a fly larva slinked its way out from under one wafer, as if to say hello, and then disappeared again into the lower depths of the ciborium. I was horrified. This was the body of Christ. What was to be done? How could one deal with such a desecration? I returned the ciborium to the tabernacle (the place where consecrated bread is kept) and, feeling unable to tell the presiding priest at the Mass, rushed to find my novice master. Father Luke was unflustered by the news. He explained I could either burn the contents of the ciborium, or dissolve the hosts in water and pour the liquefied consecrated matter down the sacrarium (the sacristy's drain), which went directly into the ground. When I blanched at the thought of doing either, he walked me back to the sacristy (the chapel's preparation room), sat me down in a chair and allowed me to watch as he placed the hosts in a large glass jar, filled it with water, and reaching into the jar with his hand and stirred it until the wafers had dissolved. It all disappeared down the sacrarium and the consecrated matter poured into the earth below.

That experience is not etched on my memory as superstitious fear. It was an occasion when Christ's sacramental presence so filled me with awe that I could not do what circumstance required. My religious imagination—altered by monastic formation—had reshaped my sense of the physical world and filled me with a new and wonderful awareness of God's presence in the world. What had been an incomprehensible doctrine for me as I prepared to become a Catholic had, in a few short years, become a living reality that shaped my experience of God's presence in the world.

How has the first element of religion shaped your experience of faith? In what ways does it continue to guide your religious practice? When reflecting on this, remember that the Child's Way is not limited to your biological childhood but also reflects other periods of intense religious formation, like preparations for the Rite of Christian Initiation for Adults (RCIA) or the early years of life in a religious order. This element is one dominated by external, authoritative, historical, traditional, and institutional aspects of your faith experience.

Roman Catholics immediately identify these adjectives with the hierarchical structures of the Church. From the pope and bishops, who have the task of teaching and resolving questions of faith and practice, Catholics have an external, authoritative, institutional structure that is reinforced by traditional practices and beliefs with historical roots stretching back more than two thousand years. This is a heritage cherished inside the Church and envied by many who view it from a distance. These structures have provided a sense of stability and order—some might even say certainty—that engenders trust in the truth claims of Roman Catholicism.

Yet few of us come to knowledge of Christian belief and practice through the pope or our local bishop. For most of us this formation is received from parents and family, the parish school of religion, an influential priest, or at Mass. Over the last two decades the *Catechism of the Catholic Church* has become the go-to text for most questions about Catholic teaching. Bishops cite it as the authoritative judgment on a wide range of subjects. It has enabled a Church of well over a billion adherents to maintain a consistent voice across continents, cultures, and countries. Before the Second Vatican Council, many Catholics took pride in the fact that one could enter a Catholic Church in any part of the world and be immediately at home because the Latin liturgy was the same everywhere.

There is much that is good and positive about these experiences. This childlike trust calls to mind the easy beautiful innocence of the Garden of Eden in Genesis 2, in which the Creator God provided all that Adam needed. God directed his life and sought his good. All man needed to do in return was listen, obey, and trust God's words to be true. When I read that text I feel a wistful longing for a simpler way of living, in which trusted authorities could be depended upon to guide me in all the ways I need to go.

I recall toward the end of my novitiate speaking with a seminary professor who asked about my experience of monastic formation. I stated with some passion that I did not want this stage of monastic life to end. I had gratefully given up my own will and wanted to be armed with "the strong and most excellent arms of obedience to do battle for Christ the Lord, the true king."[2]

Being joined to my community in simple vows proved a joyous occasion, unalloyed by regret or fear. Like the first humans at the end of Genesis 2, I had been stripped of all that had mattered outside the monastery. I felt no shame, for my eyes were on God's presence in our midst. I recall going to bed the night I took my first vows, hoping that this interior

---

2 Rule of Saint Benedict, Prologue.

peace would never end. If I only remained obedient and pliable to the authorities in my life, all would be well.

But as we all know, lurching on the edges of this longing are the realities of human life, whether in families, church, religious life, or our experiences of "the world." The Child's Way is not the destination of our journey of faith but a starting point. Because this element of belief is so dependent on the earliest religious influences in our lives, we may discover ourselves on a path that does not reflect God's best for our lives. In the next chapter we will consider what can happen when we find ourselves questioning the spiritual path we were led down in the Child's Way. How should we respond? This is not an easy or pleasant part of the journey of faith but one that may require us to ask hard questions. It may also call for courage to act on newly understood truths about our faith.

Meditation

I hold this still: I am a Catholic by virtue of my believing in a God; and if I am asked why I believe in a God, I answer that it is because I believe in myself, for I feel it impossible to believe in my own existence (and of that fact I am quite sure) without believing also in the existence of Him who lives as a Personal, All-seeing, All-judging Being in my conscience.

JOHN HENRY NEWMAN
APOLOGIA PRO VITA SUA (1865), 198

CHAPTER TWO

Difficulties of the Child's Way

To the end of the longest life you are still a beginner.
What Christ asks of you is not sinlessness,
but diligence.

JOHN HENRY NEWMAN
PAROCHIAL AND PLAIN SERMONS (1840), 5:61

In the opening pages of his autobiography, John Henry Newman described the negative power of the first element of belief over the religious imagination of an adult Christian. As a sixty-three-year-old man, he looked back on his fifteen- and forty-two-year-old selves and observed:

> *Now I come to two...[books] which produced a deep impression on me...when I was fifteen years old, each contrary to each, and planting in me the seeds of an intellectual inconsistency which disabled me for a long course of years. I read Joseph Milner's Church History, and was nothing short of enamoured of the long extracts from Saint Augustine, Saint Ambrose, and the other Fathers which I found there. I read them as being the religion of the primitive Christians: but simultaneously with Milner I read Newton on the Prophecies, and in consequence became most firmly convinced that the Pope was the Antichrist predicted by Daniel, Saint Paul, and Saint John. My imagination was stained by the effects of this doctrine up to the year 1843.*

His belief that the pope was the Antichrist "had been obliterated from my reason and judgment at an earlier date; but the thought remained upon me as a sort of false conscience." What he knew through his reason and judgment as a mature theologian struggled to overcome the power of a religious imagination formed at age fifteen. Newman only resolved it after "many years of intellectual unrest" and only after a "gradual decay and extinction."

Here we have the autobiographical reflections of a great nineteenth-century Anglican theologian who converted to Roman Catholicism at age forty-five, describing the slow and painful death of a belief he had received in the early years of his faith. Though he had intellectually settled the question years before, a "false conscience" disabled Newman for many years. This is the power of the religious imagination formed in your earliest years. While it can be a source of strength and stability, a malformed religious imagination can be a hindrance to growth and maturity in faith.

When I look back at my early life growing up in the American South during the 1950s and 1960s, a theological justification for racism stained my religious imagination well into adulthood. Though my preacher father had made a decision to teach in historically black universities after finishing his doctorate at Duke University—and never promoted racial prejudice in private conversation or from his pulpit—I learned in the schoolyard of the Appalachian town of my birth that African Americans were inferior to whites. Adults I respected spoke casually of the scriptural basis for the subordination of the "Negro" (when people spoke politely), and witnessed Ku Klux Klan rallies along the roadside on evening drives to my grandparents. Among my earliest memories are separate water fountains for whites and blacks, and experiences of gas station restrooms being rudely forbidden to African American families.

All of this was justified, many people thought, because of the curse of Ham (Genesis 9:20–27). In this Genesis account, Noah cursed Ham's son, Canaan, because Ham had looked on the drunken nakedness of his father and joked about it to his brothers. Ham was thought to be the father of the dark-skinned races, which had inherited his curse. Sadly, this became the dominant justification for slavery in the United States during the nineteenth century.

One of my doctoral students, Hudson Davis, prepared a significant study that explains another "biblically grounded" justification for American racism, which also misconstrued the words of Scripture. This ill-informed theory rested on Bible commentator Adam Clarke's mistaken assertion that the Hebrew word for "serpent" in the temptation account of the Garden of Eden (Genesis 3:1) was better rendered as "ape" or "orangutan." Building on this mistaken notion, mid-nineteenth-century racial theorists speculated that the tempter of Adam and Eve must have been a "Negro" gardener. This not only subjected the "Negro" to a divine curse but also relegated the "Negro" to a beast of the field and not a descendant of Adam.

Religiously grounded fears of the free "Negro" inspired Jim Crow laws in the Southern states and the mass incarceration of African American men. They also formed the premise for laws against interracial marriage, as well as lynchings and the periodic violent attacks on black communities. This misuse of Scripture to dehumanize African Americans has had a long life and continues to be promoted by white supremacist and Christian identity groups even today. When one recalls the Memphis sanitation workers' strike in 1968 and the placards they wore which read, "I am a Man," the tragedy of this false use of Scripture deepens. Today too, the association of African Americans with apes in the humor of some Americans sadly remains alive and well. For someone like me, a son of the South (born the year of Brown v. Board of Education, 1954), Dr. Davis' study of this racist theology of "Negro" origins has been strangely liberating. To understand that a false logic premised what I had always assumed was an irrational conditioning in childhood means that I can now explain it, call it what it is, and move on. Knowledge is a powerful thing. Yet like Newman, I am aware that knowledge is not enough.

Though sensitive to the plight of African Americans during the Civil Rights era of the 1960s, I struggled with this stain on my religious imagination. A "false conscience" influenced every interaction I had with African Americans, long after I knew and understood the root cause of this prejudice. A distorted use of sacred Scripture had justified this oppression and misuse of African Americans for centuries. Yet it took more than knowledge to reshape my attitude. Only a changed heart and conscious refusal to act on this deeply ingrained notion caused this stain on my religious imagination to wither. While I now can function without this "false conscience," it remains a great sorrow that too many Americans still struggle with this prejudice and perpetuate this wrong.

Are there stains on your religious imagination? Have you discovered a false conscience that limits your ability to respond with Christian charity and compassion to people you have been taught to think of as "other," or repugnant to God? Being able to identify these areas of your religious imagination is one thing. Letting go of them and experiencing an interior transformation is quite another matter.

Within Christian ecclesial communities, it is possible for the first element of religion to dominate to such an extent that tradition and historic practices impair the church and render it unable to do what is necessary to flourish...and even survive. Perhaps the most tragic example of the fatal consequences of rigid conformity to tradition is the death of the Nubian Church.

In 1742, a Franciscan friar reported to Rome the remarkable news that a hitherto unknown Christian community had been discovered on a Nile River island in Nubia, the region south of what once had been Roman Egypt. The ancient Nubian Church, established no later than the fourth century, had persevered through the first millennium of Islam, despite periods of isolation from the patriarchate of Alexandria, which had traditionally supplied it with bishops. But the Nubian Church had been thought extinct for centuries, cut off as it was from other Christian communions. Pondering the fate of the Nubian Church, the Franciscan posed a rhetorical question: "How did Nubia go astray from the Christian faith?" His answer was surprising and unequivocal: "Only because of a lack of pastors."

The Nubian laity had struggled to keep the faith. In the early 1500s, a Syrian traveler reported finding more than 150 well-tended churches in Nubia, with crucifixes, altars, and images of the Blessed Virgin. While the people were not Christian, Muslim, or Jewish, the traveler found they lived with the desire of being Christians. In the 1520s, six Nubian lay Christians traveled south to Ethiopia and begged the emperor for priests and monks. But the Ethiopian Church was struggling with its own challenge. It also depended on Alexandria for its bishop, and after decades without a bishop, the Ethiopians had an aging and dying clergy. So the emperor sent the Nubians away. Their church died for a lack of pastors. By 1742, only a stray remnant of that once-thriving ancient church remained.

The Nubian people had carried on for generations with their desire to be Christian, but church leadership had failed them. No doubt these leaders were sincere and well-meaning. Bishops had always come from Alexandria, and priestly ordination depended on these bishops. But when circumstances changed, the structures intended to supply pastoral care and evangelical witness failed to adapt. Preserving customary ecclesiastical discipline took precedence over spreading the good news and nurturing the faithful with word and sacraments. It was not Islam that destroyed Nubian Christianity.

By failing to provide nurturing pastoral care and sacramental ministry, church leaders starved the faith of lay people who desired to live as Christians.

When you look back on your own early formation and the religious imagination cultivated by the authorities in your life, were you formed in perfect truth and practice? Or did that formation create—in one or more areas—a false conscience that distorted your faith and understanding of the world? Because each person's life experience is unique, the first element of belief is different for everyone. While impressions of religious truth conveyed by authorities may be sources of growth in faith, these same authorities also have the capacity to contort religious faith and practice, and derail the best principles of our Christian tradition.

We live in an age when media no longer shields us from the faults and failures of religious leaders. Televangelists and megachurch pastors who rail against adultery and homosexuality are exposed for engaging in these very acts. Prosperity gospel preachers who call on their faithful to make tithes and offerings beyond financial prudence are caught embezzling those very funds intended for God's work.

In the Roman Catholic Church we have lived with the painful, unfolding story of clerical sexual abuse of minors and vulnerable adults. Though we know that this is a tragic reality in all ecclesial communities and religious traditions, the fact that so many bishops have failed to protect the most vulnerable among us has been an unrelenting scandal and source of disillusionment for many faithful Catholics.

A distressing struggle can be discerned among Catholics whose faith is dominated by the first element of belief. For some, the need to respect and revere church authorities has been greater than a call for compassion and justice for victims. I have even met Catholics who deny that priests or bishops have engaged in these abuses, for their ordination sets them apart and endows them with special grace. Even among those who acknowledge the facts, some seek to justify the silence and concealment of these acts (particularly the bishops who have not disciplined pedophile priests, or shielded the faithful from knowledge of their acts). They argue that the authority of the Church is at stake. For these Catholics, it is easier to disbelieve the news or criticize the victims speaking out than to accept the sad truth of the betrayal of vows and the failures of Church leaders.

For other Catholics who have functioned primarily in the first element of belief, this reality has been a faith-shattering event. When these believers received this news, the trust and obedience on which their faith had depended was destroyed. These Catholics lost confidence that bishops and priests model the gospel and proclaim God's truth. Living in the first element of belief uncritically, they have been left with a sense of betrayal and loss. They feel bereft and do not know where to turn.

If faith is to grow and mature, life experience demands that we confront the humanity of religious authorities in our lives and appreciate the fallibility of the religious institutions they govern. Do you recall when you first questioned the religious authorities in your life? What experience or series of events first drew your mind to the possibility that the religious authorities in your life might be fallible? When did you realize aspects of your belief system might require a critical reassessment because of new experiences or an insight gained from an unexpected source?

For faith to achieve greater balance, the Youth's Way—that questioning, argumentative, reasoning element of belief—must play a role in our lives and communities. The next two chapters focus on the Youth's Way. They explore how the second element of belief can play a positive role in your experience of faith and consider the challenges that it may present to you as a believer.

Meditation

As neither the local rulers nor the pastors of the Church are impeccable [sinless] in act or infallible in judgment, I am not obliged to maintain that all ecclesiastical measures and permissions have ever been praiseworthy.

JOHN HENRY NEWMAN
VIA MEDIA, I (PREFACE, 1877)

A people's religion is ever a corrupt religion, in spite of the provisions of Holy Church. If she is to be Catholic, you must admit within her net fish of every kind, guests good and bad, vessels of gold, vessels of earth.

JOHN HENRY NEWMAN
CERTAIN DIFFICULTIES FELT BY ANGLICANS (1876) 1:81

SECTION II

The Second Element of Belief

CHAPTER THREE

Faith Seeking Understanding

Brothers and sisters, do not be children in your thinking ...but in thinking be adults.

1 CORINTHIANS 14:20

I know that even the unaided reason, when correctly exercised, leads to a belief in God.

JOHN HENRY NEWMAN
APOLOGIA PRO VITA SUA (1865), 380

In Newman's lectures on the Idea of a University he observed, "When the intellect has once been properly trained and formed to have a connected view or grasp of things, it will display its powers with more or less effect according to its particular quality and capacity in the individual. In the case of most [people] it makes itself felt in the good sense, sobriety of thought, reasonableness, candour, self-command, and steadiness of view [which characterize each person]." Newman recognized rational development as necessary for human growth and influence in the world. He noted that an educated person whose views reflect only partial truths or even falsehoods inspire more respect than a "mere hereditary Christian who has never realized [understood] the truths which he holds, [and] is able to do nothing [with them]."

In order to become a person of faith in the fullest sense, you must exercise your reason, ask questions, search for answers, and take seriously experiences of doubt that you encounter on your spiritual journey. This inquisitive element of belief is not a threat to your Christian life. In fact, failure to embrace it may well result in a loss of faith. Your rational capacity is an essential part of the image of God in you. I take comfort in the gospel accounts of how Jesus' disciples doubted the resurrection. If those who were closest to him and heard his teachings firsthand had their struggles, why should you be different? Yet as you grow in the second element of belief, do not expect to be praised for exercising it. The authorities of your Child's Way may well treat your questions as threatening or as acts of defiance. My experience of the emerging second element of belief was not easy or smooth. It actually brought much pain for me and for those I loved most.

When I was around the age of fourteen, my parents discovered that I had been browsing the religion section of our town's only bookstore and had been purchasing handbooks on Hinduism, Buddhism, and other world religions. Since childhood I had been fascinated by ancient religious systems. Dad and Mother had tolerated my curiosity about the dead religions of the Greeks, Romans, and Nordic peoples, and even took pride in my precocious reading habits. Studying Greco-Roman myths and exploring the legends of Norse gods seemed a harmless pastime. Living religions were another matter. This curiosity no doubt sparked parental fears of apostasy or loss of faith in Christianity. My father took me aside and told me firmly that I did not need to read books about these traditions. He could tell me all I needed to know.

While most of what I knew about Christianity had come from my father's preaching, my fourteen-year-old self knew that Dad did not have the experience or knowledge to satisfy my curiosity about other religious traditions. By that time I had a Jewish friend and had visited his synagogue. During travels in the Middle East with my parents I had been inside mosques and witnessed Islamic prayers.

Several years later a visually impaired Christian Scientist friend whom I had helped one summer gave me Herman Hesse's *Siddhartha* (a novel that retells the life of the Buddha). When I described to my mother moving passages that contained (for me) spiritual insights, Mother asked, "Is the author a Christian?" When I said no, she remarked, "A non-Christian has nothing meaningful to say to a believer." It was a striking moment, for it confirmed how different my way of viewing the world had become.

Despite my parents' best attempts, life experience, new friendships, and my wide-ranging reading began to open new vistas and call into doubt deeply ingrained assumptions I had about the Christian faith and the world that I had received from childhood authorities. Ironically, it was their efforts to expose me to the world through travel and education that had opened my eyes to other ways of worship and other belief systems. With that larger context in mind, it was hard *not* to perceive that Christianity was bigger than the tradition of my childhood. It was hard *not* to be aware that other religious traditions had insights into the mystery of God's loving presence in our world.

When did you begin to question the beliefs and practices of your childhood? What experiences caused you to puzzle over the trustworthiness of the immovable markers of your religious landscape? How did the authorities in your life react or respond when you began to ask for reasons to believe, rather than submit in childlike obedience? Did they treat these queries as trustful questioning or as signs of creeping apostasy, skepticism, or defiance?

For Catholics of a certain age, their second element of

belief collectively began with the striking contrast between the ethos of the Catholic Church prior to Vatican II, and the change (and turmoil) that followed the council. When Pope John XXIII said, "I want to throw open the windows of the Church so that we can see out and the people can see in," many experienced it as permission to ask long-suppressed questions and pursue knowledge that had been restricted—even forbidden. Liturgy in the vernacular, encouragement to read the Bible, permission to visit non-Catholic places of worship… these are just the beginning of a long list of startling alterations in the religious landscape for Catholics. In the Catholic Church—with its strong, centralized structures of authority—this rapid change in ethos became a tempting occasion to ignore and even rebel against Church leaders. This is often the struggle, when individuals and communities of faith face the perplexing challenge of humanity's capacity to reason, ask questions, and even criticize authorities who have dominated their first element experience of belief.

When we look at the opening chapters of the Bible, it is evident that this challenge has existed since the beginning of human consciousness. Genesis 2 and 3 are where we normally start any discussion of sin in the world. While not detracting from this principal interpretation, it is important to reflect on another layer of meaning in these passages that illustrate the second element of belief.

Adam and Eve lived in a garden that contained all that human life required and much to delight and comfort the human body and spirit. Yet we know—even in the untroubled context of the second chapter of Genesis—that at the center of that garden was the perplexing, nagging desire to acquire knowledge that goes beyond what can be perceived through the senses or mediated through divine authority. Even though God had told man that eating of the tree of knowledge of good and evil brought a fearsome consequence, human curiosity drew Adam and Eve to that part of the garden, and they contemplated the possibilities of what that knowledge might mean in their lives.

Years ago I studied Genesis 2 and 3 and explored how commentators have approached these texts. While we are all familiar with dominant interpretations of Genesis 3 and the assumptions that link the serpent with Revelation 12:9 (suggesting a Satanic presence in the Garden of Eden), less familiar ways of interpreting this text have not treated the serpent as inherently evil. Instead, the serpent is identified with human curiosity and the emerging awareness of humanity's capacity to choose.

We should consider these passages carefully, for they get at the core of the second element of belief. The tree of knowledge of good and evil is the place to start:

> And the LORD God commanded the man, "you may freely eat of every tree of the garden; but of the tree of

knowledge of good and evil you shall not eat, For in the day that you eat of it you shall die."

GENESIS 2:16–17

When eighteen-year-old freshmen take my introduction to theology class, they are bothered by these verses. What kind of father is this Creator God? He makes a beautiful garden, places man and woman there and then puts right at the center a tree that cannot be touched without incurring death. These students rail about this arbitrary and unjust punishment. If God really loved Adam and Eve, God would forgive them and give them a second chance. Some argue that if God really wanted obedience, God should not have created the tree of knowledge of good and evil. Others object: How could human beings exercise "freedom" and "choice" without that tree? Still others say, "God doesn't have to threaten to kill them to make the point."

My eighteen-year-old students are not arguing in the abstract. They struggle with this question in real life, after almost two decades of parental care. They cannot consider the tree of knowledge of good and evil without thinking about "sex" and a hundred other things that parents forbid with the penalty of "death."

Before fatherhood I have to admit that the tree at the center of the garden looked arbitrary and tricky to me as well. Now—as a father—I realize that the tree represents the hope all loving parents have: that their children will listen to their instructions and avoid things in life that cause suffering.

When my eldest was not yet twenty months old, he enjoyed toddling around in the mornings while his mother savored a cup of hot tea. Every morning he rushed over to see the contents and every morning his mother would say gently, and then with increasing sternness, "hot tea, no, no!" Being a smart and curious baby, he awaited his opportunity, and one morning as his mother and I focused on plans for the day, he moved in and grabbed the cup. Hot liquid spilled on his hands and arms as he cried with pain. All we could do was comfort him. He became withdrawn for a time and avoided our embraces. The next morning when I brought the cup of tea, my son looked up at the cup and shouted, "hot tea, no, no!" Through his choices, he had discovered what we had sought to keep from him as long as possible. Yet despite our best efforts, he gained knowledge of the world that changed him. He had come to know, through suffering and loss of innocence, something he would have never understood through obedience.

Perhaps this is what Saint Benedict meant in the opening paragraph of the Prologue when he stated, "that by the toil of obedience thou mayest return to Him from whom by the sloth of disobedience thou has gone away." While Benedict frames it with a harsh judgment—sloth of disobedience—this return to a more perfect submission to God's will is only possible because the monk "knows" the consequences of "disobedience," or failure to live by God's precepts.

I can appreciate the emotional vigor of a parent who shouts, "If you do that I'll kill you." It's not about anger or rage at disobedience—but a momentary primordial fear that causes a parent to invoke the ultimate consequence to deter harm. Yet it is only the most demented and disturbed parent that acts on this impulse. Like any loving parent, the Creator Father instills dread of his authority to divert the child from making choices that will cause suffering, pain, or harm.

> Now the serpent was more crafty than any other wild animal that the LORD God had made.
>
> GENESIS 3:1A

The "serpent" is a fascinating religious symbol. It is significant in almost all ancient cultures, even those separated by oceans, deserts, and mountains. From the Northern and Southern hemispheres to the Eastern and Western hemispheres humans have been obsessed with the serpent as a symbol of life's mysteries. These serpent symbols have been positive, ambiguous, or downright villainous. Could it be that the serpent and the tree of knowledge of good and evil represent our human capacity to be like the Creator God, making choices that shape our world?

> He said to the woman, "Did God say, 'You shall not eat of any tree in the garden?'"
>
> GENESIS 3:1B

This translation presents the serpent's question in an excluding way (did God forbid any fruit to be eaten?). The King James translates the question more inclusively, "Ye shall not eat of every tree of the garden?" The serpent asks woman: isn't everything permitted?

> The woman said to the serpent, "We may eat of the fruit of the trees in the garden; but God said, 'You shall not eat of the fruit of the tree that is in the middle of the garden, nor shall you touch it, or you shall die.'"
>
> GENESIS 3:2–3

The woman's reply is accurate in its scope and detail. She confirmed that man and woman may eat any of the fruits of the garden. There was no limit on the choices man and woman could make. Yet God made a distinction in the consequences that follow from the choices made. All the trees of the garden, including the tree of life, could be eaten with a positive outcome—man and woman would be nourished and sustained. The tree of knowledge of good and evil proved the sole exception.

> But the serpent said to the woman, "You will not die;for God knows that when you eat of ityour eyes will be opened, and you will be like God (gods), knowing good and evil."
>
> GENESIS 3:4–5

The irony is that the serpent was right—she would not drop dead. But life did change. She made a choice to seek knowledge of good and evil. And she would live with the consequences of that choice.

> So when the woman saw that the tree was good for food, and that it was a delight to the eyes, and that the tree was to be desired to make one wise, she took of its fruit and ate, and she also gave some to her husband, who was with her, and he ate.
>
> GENESIS 3:6

Note that she engaged in a reasoning process. Though the Father Creator issued a dire warning of an extreme consequence, woman saw that the tree was good for food (like the other trees of the garden), that it was pleasing to the eye (like the rest of the fruit in the garden), and that eating it would impart knowledge that only her Creator Father possessed. She made a choice. She ate the fruit and encouraged man to do the same.

✣ ✣ ✣

As if viewing a film, I would like for us to press the pause button and reflect on this moment in the experience of these archetypal humans. Prior to that choice, living in childlike obedience to their Creator Father had been—from all we are told—a life of blissful relationship with God. God had placed them in a beautiful garden with all that they required for a healthy life. The archetypal couple had a steward's role...useful occupation caring for a garden that easily yielded its fruits for their physical needs. The only prohibition placed on them was to avoid tasting the fruit of knowledge of good and evil.

Yet woman and man, created as they were in the image of God, responded to the beauty of the fruit, recognized its potential—like the other fruits of the garden—to nourish them, and realized it had the power to make them more like their Creator Father. One can imagine that woman (and man) might well have reasoned that this fruit could even strengthen the bond between them and God, for by eating it they would become even more like the God they loved.

I certainly recall those thoughts in my teenage years, when at various stages I struggled over whether to obey my parents and live within the parameters of their "garden." However, this is not simply an adolescent struggle. We all live in relationships that define and confine our scope of action. In marriage, obedience and conformity to spousal expectations is essential for a harmonious life. Monks live under obedience to their abbot, and priests live under obedience to their bishop.

Yet there remains that reasoning, questioning part of ourselves that cannot, will not be denied. Even in the most compliant person there remains the interior struggle to ask the questions that puzzle us, chafe at the parameters that seem to limit our lives, and contemplate new horizons as they come to our consciousness. The choices we make in the midst of this second element of belief often are life-changing and unalterable. Some can be harmful and destroy much that is good in our lives and the experience of those who are touched by our choices.

The impact of these choices is what we must explore in our next chapter. As you read it, consider how that argumentative, questioning part of you has functioned in your life of faith. What rational, philosophical systems have shaped the religious path you have followed? While there is much to praise in this second element of belief, it is volatile and dangerous.

Yet it is this aspect that sets us apart in the created order. It is not to be vilified. It must be nurtured and used for our growth as people of faith. Like Saint Thomas in the Gospel of John (20:24–29), we may find some things are hard to believe. When Christ appeared to him, Thomas was not rebuked for his doubts but offered proof and invited to touch Christ's wounds. When he professed Jesus to be his Lord and God, Christ responded, "Blessed are those who have not seen and yet have come to believe."

Meditation

The Rationalist makes himself his own centre, not his Maker; he does not go to God, but he implies that God must come to him. And this, it is to be feared, is the spirit in which multitudes of us act at the present day.

JOHN HENRY NEWMAN, *TRACT 73: ON THE INTRODUCTION OF RATIONALISTIC PRINCIPLES INTO REVEALED RELIGION* (1836)

CHAPTER FOUR

Struggles of the Youth's Way

Do not suppose I have been speaking in disparagement of human reason: It is the way to faith; Its conclusions are often the very objects of faith... But still reason is one thing and faith is another, And reason can as little be made a substitute for faith, As faith can be made a substitute for reason.

JOHN HENRY NEWMAN
DISCOURSES ADDRESSED TO MIXED CONGREGATIONS
(1881), 189

In David Lodge's 1965 novel *The British Museum is Falling Down*, he recounted one day in the life of Adam Appleby (note the name!), a twenty-five-year-old married Catholic man studying English literature at the University of London during the Second Vatican Council (1962–1965). Adam's morning began with amorous musings as his wife measured her body temperature and recorded it on a Church-sponsored calendar to determine her "safe period," while their three young children toddled about, reminding him of the fruits of impetuous marital union. When his wife reported symptoms of morning sickness, Adam was filled with dread.

As he scootered his way to the British Museum for a day of research, Adam encountered his parish priest, Father Finbar, and offered him a lift. Just after a near accident on a busy London street—Adam's attention distracted by fearful thoughts of a fourth pregnancy after four years of marriage—he blurted out to the good Irish priest, "Do you think the council will change the Church's attitude on birth control?" Father Finbar stiffened and responded with absolute certainty, "The Church's teaching never changes...on that or any other matter." Being an educated layman, Adam countered with John Henry Newman's theory of doctrinal development. To this Father Finbar reacted, "Newman, wasn't he a Protestant?"

Blessed John Henry Newman's spiritual journey took him beyond his first forty-five years as a Protestant, and his theory of doctrinal development (written during his last troubled years as a Protestant) proved greater than one individual's private intellectual quest to convert to Roman Catholicism. While it has been mistakenly reported many times that Pope Paul VI called Vatican II Newman's council, it is true that the pope credited Newman with raising questions pertinent for the times: ecumenism (dialogue with other Christians), the role of laity in the life of the Church, the relationship between Christianity and the world, and how Christians should engage non-Christian religions.

Because he was a man known for asking intelligent questions, Pope Paul VI called the era of the council and its aftermath "Newman's hour."[3] For that pope and his predecessor, the second element of religion was no longer optional in that season of the Church's life. It was a necessity. When John XXIII opened the windows of the Church, new vistas created a space for questions to be asked and new possibilities to be tested. Yet dangers lurched in the shadowy valleys not just for the questioners but also for authorities charged with defending systems of belief and codes of conduct.

Adam Appleby's question about birth control was a trustful question from an obedient (albeit frustrated) Catholic. Father Finbar's response might have been sufficient prior to Vatican II—in an ethos many lay Catholics experienced as dominated by the first element of belief. Yet it proved inadequate for a

3 L'Osservatore Romano (English edition), April 17, 1975 (368).

new generation of educated, intellectually curious lay people, who—armed with conciliar documents about their role in the Church—wanted more than assertions of unalterable truth. They wanted intellectual engagement that might satisfy *their* questions. In an era when church authority appeared to be swiftly changing the liturgy, thought, and practices of the Church—often with little explanation—this seemed a reasonable expectation.

It was this questioning Church, struggling to understand its place in the world—among other Christians and other peoples of faith—that I encountered in the 1970s. Particularly among the monks I came to know at Saint Andrew's Abbey, these new opportunities and pressing questions seemed to be matters they relished. Father Vincent had an active dialogue with the Jewish community of Los Angeles, and Father Thaddeus met frequently with Buddhists. Brother Peter thrived among Evangelical Protestants at Fuller Seminary, and Father Francis regularly said Masses for Charismatic Catholic fellowships. Father Eleutharius taught philosophy at the Claremont Graduate School and loved to engage students and faculty on the intersection between contemporary philosophy and the Catholic tradition.

I mention all this because it was a dynamic ethos and a reinvigorated spirit that a non-Catholic like me could sense and admire. Yet it was also evident that Catholics around the world struggled between obedience and newfound freedoms, between tradition and a yearning for change. Some Catholics complained that the renewal had gone too far, while others fumed that it had not gone far enough. Archbishop Marcel Lefebvre and his traditionalist Society of Saint Pius X broke with the Church and condemned the decrees of the council as innovations. At the other end of the spectrum certain liberation theologians criticized Church leaders for complicity with repressive governments, sought to interpret the Christian message through Marxist principles and joined armed resistance movements to end political oppression.

I think about this a great deal these days because I am living these developments in the microcosm of my home. When I look at my own sons—two who are already teenagers and another one who will soon follow—discussions about their beliefs and right conduct are at times disconcerting. Though we pray together and have ongoing casual conversations about our faith, it is clear that their life experiences are causing them to test ideas and try on ways of thinking about the mysteries of our faith that do not align perfectly with their father's faith. One of my boys concluded after a discussion of transubstantiation that Catholics are cannibals. During a presentation about the resurrected Jesus at a catechetical class I teach, my eldest observed that Jesus was the original zombie (other students—well-versed in the horror-film genre—loved it). My youngest takes pleasure in observing that he believes in reincarnation. When I point out that this is a Hindu and not a Christian belief, he shrugs and smiles. What is a father to do—thunder from the heights and make my sons fear to speak their minds? Or should I allow a space to exist where conversation and influence can continue to be exercised over time?

There are times when I have confrontations—a clash of wills—with my sons. These can be quite heated, as I stake out a position that I know is best for their well-being and the good of our family. Beyond a certain point I lose patience and am tempted to say, "Do it" or "Don't do it" because I say so. After all, I am (for at least a few more months!) the biggest guy in the room.

Instead, I name what they are doing. They are not listening to my counsel and resisting my judgment. I tell them (sometimes harshly) that they clearly think they know best, and they should act on their judgment and not mine. I walk away and leave them to consider the choice they seem determined to make. Remarkably, in most instances they opt to be in accord with me rather than to act on their own will. They crave to be in harmony with their father. But I know this will not be the case forever.

I take comfort in knowing that my experience resembles that of the Creator God of Genesis. In the previous chapter we considered the fateful account of woman and man in Genesis 3. I would like to pick up where we left off. For the next verses speak to the consequences of choices made.

> Then the eyes of them both were opened, and they knew that they were naked;and they sewed fig leaves togetherand made loincloths for themselves.
>
> GENESIS 3:7

Knowledge is a double-edged sword. When we pursue it we often find that it reveals aspects of life—of ourselves—that we did not know existed and regret having discovered. We may attempt to conceal this new knowledge from others—and ourselves—but it changes us and alters the crucial relationships in our lives.

> They heard the sound of the LORD God walking in the garden at the time of the evening breeze, and the man and his wife hid themselves from the presence of the LORD God among the trees of the garden.
>
> GENESIS 3:8

This passage is at once the most beautiful and one of the saddest in all of Scripture. God came at the usual time, in the cool of the evening, and they did not run to greet him, but hid instead.

Has this ever happened to you? I certainly recognize this reaction. During times when I have sought knowledge on my own terms, I have discovered in my willfulness not only things that I do not want to know about myself and the world but also have felt alienated from God and those I love most.

I act on that alienation and create the breach by avoiding communion with God and evading the kindness of those who love me best. It is not God who judges us but we who condemn ourselves.

> But the LORD God called to the man, and said to him, "Where are you?" He said, "I heard the sound of you in the garden, and I was afraid, because I was naked; and I hid myself."
>
> GENESIS 3:9–10

This passage brings back haunting memories of my earthly father. He was a larger-than-life presence for me. He seemed to be into everything. Dad was a pastor, a professor, and a successful businessman. This meant that he often left home before I woke and returned after I had gone to bed. Yet I knew that he constantly thought of how to make a way for me in the world. After high school he placed me in my own personal Eden, for he knew I loved learning. I studied at the best college within the tradition of my birth, and he only asked that I call him each Sunday around lunchtime, for it was the one time during the week that he was sure to be home.

These calls became a trial for me because they coincided with a period when I lost the faith of my childhood. As I stopped going to the local church and stayed in bed, I had to deal with Dad's perfunctory questions about the services he thought I was attending. I became very good at diverting his attention, keeping the conversation focused on *his* morning and the sermon *he* had delivered. He enjoyed my interest in his work. What a dutiful son, he thought.

When I started attending services in other churches, he never found out, never suspected what I hid from him. Then during a joyous period, when in the context of a little Episcopal church, I discovered the richness of liturgical worship and learned from the Anglo-Catholic priest the power of sacraments, I had to conceal that, too. Dad would never understand. I hid in the garden Dad had created for me and lived with the misery of knowing that someday he would find out...which of course he did.

The pain of that experience rivaled that of man and woman in the garden (or so I imagined), and I did what they did. I blamed others, even my benefactor father, and refused to accept responsibility for the fact that in pursuing my own path I had engaged in conduct that alienated me from the father I loved.

Yet like the Creator Father of Genesis 3, my father did not kill me. Instead, he dealt with his disappointment and the new reality. He continued to provide for my needs and helped prepare me for the world outside the garden he had intended for me. He knew that I would go my own way. But he loved me anyway. One of my uncles told me of his agony and the temptation to punish me by withholding support on which my studies depended. Yet he concluded, "how can I withhold from my son what I am able to give?"

Years later, in the wake of my conversion to Roman Catholicism (which truly broke his heart), Dad and I had a memorable conversation. He expressed a grudging respect for the fact that I had asked hard questions of myself and of my faith. I had made choices that were authentically mine. He could see that I had become my own man and would make my own way in the world. I was his dependent no longer.

That conversation proved a special grace, for four weeks later—and three days after I defended my doctoral dissertation—Dad died when the plane he was piloting suddenly lost altitude and crashed on a busy street in Greensboro, North Carolina. That event became my exile from the garden Dad had created for me, for the consequences of my choices continue to mark my life and the lives of my children.

The second element of belief is a great gift, but it comes at a price. Yet this element of belief, like the first element, is not sufficient in itself. For faith to grow and mature, we must take a further step, beyond the authorities who guide our lives, and past the abilities of our reason to raise questions, explore systems of knowledge, and draw conclusions based on our own analysis.

We must next consider how the third element of belief plays its role in the life of a Christian. What is the Adult's Way? How does the ethico-mystical element function in the maturing Christian? This third element of belief assumes a firm place in your life when the human limits of your authorities become evident and the capacity of your reason to critically analyze truth claims is pressed beyond the bounds of rational perception. In the midst of these experiences a way forward is discovered, by acting on the deepest principles of the faith received in your first element of belief and discerned through your inquisitive second element of belief. Yet the third element may take you into uncharted territory as you explore paths that are not clearly marked by first-element authorities or discovered by the natural power of your mind. By acting on the most profound principles of your faith, you are touched by the deeper unexpected mysteries of God's presence in the world, in circumstances and places you never imagined possible. The third element of belief can transform you, as the deepest principles of faith are lived and alter your sense of who you are.

Meditation

Theology is occupied with supernatural matters and is ever running into mysteries which reason can neither explain nor adjust. Its lines of thought come to an abrupt termination and to pursue them or to complete them is to plunge down the abyss...through thick darkness and ethereal mediums.

JOHN HENRY NEWMAN
CERTAIN DIFFICULTIES FELT BY ANGLICANS (1876) 1:81

Ten thousand difficulties do not make one doubt, as I understand the subject; difficulty and doubt are incommensurate [not the same]. There of course may be difficulties in the evidence; but I am speaking of difficulties intrinsic to the doctrines, or to their compatibility with each other. A man may be annoyed that he cannot work out a mathematical problem, of which the answer is or is not given to him, without doubting that it admits of an answer, or that a particular answer is the true one.

JOHN HENRY NEWMAN,
APOLOGIA PRO VITA SUA (1865), 374

SECTION III

The Third Element of Belief

CHAPTER FIVE

Embracing the Call

Trust in the LORD with all your heart,
and do not rely on your own insight.
In all your ways acknowledge him,
and he will make straight your paths.

PROVERBS 3:5–6

What is meant by faith? It is to feel in good earnest that we are creatures of God; it is a practical perception of the unseen world; it is to understand that this world is not enough for our happiness, to look beyond it on towards God, to realize His presence, to wait upon Him, to endeavour to learn and to do His will, and to seek our good from Him. It is not a mere temporary strong act or impetuous feeling of the mind, an impression or a view coming upon it, but it is a habit, a state of mind, lasting and consistent. To have faith in God is to surrender oneself to God, humbly to put one's interests, or to wish to be allowed to put them, into His hands who is the Sovereign Giver of all good.

JOHN HENRY NEWMAN
PLAIN AND PAROCHIAL SERMONS (1837), 3:86–87

Conversio morum or conversatio morum? "Conversion of life" or "way of life?" This crucial phrase in chapter 58 of the *Rule of Saint Benedict* is one of three ancient vows made by monks, along with stability and obedience. During the early twentieth century, scholars identified an eighth-century scribal error, which for well over a millennium focused Benedictine spirituality on "*conversion* of life." Now we know that Benedict intended *conversatio morum*, which in English is commonly translated "*way* of life." This insight has been an occasion for Benedictine monks to revisit the significance of this vow, and to cultivate a renewed appreciation for their calling.

Conversion of life as a *way of life* is really at the heart of the third element of belief. It is why the Adult's Way can also be called the Ethico-Mystical Way. This element of belief focuses on an experience of faith that has been internalized and applied to your life. It is not a set of rules to be obeyed or a system of ideas to be critically evaluated but an experience of God's presence that compels you to act, to make a difference in yourself and your world. That "calling" may not always be explained by your earlier faith formation (the first element of belief), or based on rationally analyzed truth claims (second element of belief). It may seem like a flash of insight that stands in contradiction to the other elements of belief in your life up to that point, and yet....

John Henry Newman found himself in just that position in the late 1830s and early 1840s. He had been raised an Anglican as a child and formed as an evangelical in his late teens and early twenties. In those early years, Newman had been taught that no true Englishman could be a Roman Catholic. This first-element experience shaped his view of the world and himself. His early scholarship and intense intellectual life at Oriel College, Oxford, was devoted to justifying this anti-Roman Catholic attitude. He was firmly convinced that the pope was the Antichrist and that Catholics should be denied civil liberties in Great Britain. When Roman Catholics were emancipated in 1828 and gained further rights in 1832, Newman and other colleagues formed the Oxford Movement and devoted much time and effort to convince students, colleagues, and Anglicans throughout his country that the Church of England was the path to salvation. For him, the Roman Catholic Church had corrupted ancient Christian truth and endangered the spiritual health of all who lived within it.

Yet between 1839 and 1845, Newman was transformed in ways no one could have predicted. This most English of Englishmen, and most Anglican of Anglicans, experienced a series of crises—some caused by external events, others by personal study and reflection—that induced a "conversion of life" that resulted in a radically altered "way of life." After an agonizingly slow period of wrestling with his strongly developed first and second elements of belief, Newman converted to Roman Catholicism. So much about his first forty-five years of life indicated that this could never happen. And yet his willingness to be guided by the third element of belief resulted in a dramatically refashioned path for the last forty-five years of his long spiritual journey.

As inspiring as Newman's story is, you need look no further than Saint Paul in the Acts of the Apostles to find an example of how the third element of belief can dramatically alter the course of a person's life. After all, Saul (his childhood name, which means "prayed for") was a devoutly formed Jew and a highly educated Pharisee. While we are sometimes tempted to think of Pharisees only in negative terms, we must never forget that they were the spiritual athletes of Judaism in first-century Palestine. Saul was a model even among these rigorous believers. Everything about his first and second elements of belief justified the harsh stance he took toward the earliest followers of Jesus. His active persecution of Christians was an act of devotion, and given all he knew, was necessary to maintain the purity of the Jewish tradition. However, on the road to Damascus—where he planned to arrest Christians—Saul was knocked off his horse and in the midst of a blinding light had a mystical encounter with Christ that changed his life. In his blindness, Saul was led to a Damascus Christian, healed, and welcomed into the Christian community he sought to destroy. He became Paul (which means "humble") and spent the rest of his life as a passionate evangelist of the faith he had once persecuted. The third element of belief had induced a *conversion of life* that transformed his *way of life*.

However, the impact of the third element of belief is not

simply about radical conversion from one faith or church community to another. As we grow in our life of faith, new challenges and opportunities for spiritual growth become part of our journey. For me, going to prison has been that new path. Let me explain.

Watching television can change your life. This certainly happened to me one Sunday evening in April 2007, when I stretched out on the couch to watch *60 Minutes*. The opening segment was about the "Bard College Prison Initiative," a college-in-prison program started by a motivated, socially conscious undergraduate. The program showed faculty engaged in intense classroom discussions and incarcerated students arguing in the prison yard—about Hegel and Kant. The reporter described how the lives of prison students and their families had changed. Professors seemed utterly transformed. I felt compelled to act—but resisted the impulse.

I liked to think of myself as a Catholic theologian animated by the call to social justice. My Vincentian parish, Saint Vincent de Paul near downtown St. Louis, has many outreach programs and devotes much of its budget to serving those who are poor and homeless. The Jesuit commitment to justice for those at the margins gives my work at Saint Louis University direction and purpose. Yet using my teaching skills in prisons had never crossed my mind. The next day I spoke with a friend who has been in and out of prison eleven times and said, "Someone at Saint Louis University should do this.

I just don't have the time." She fixed me with a stare I could not avoid and said, "No one is too busy to do the right thing once he sees it needs to be done."

Whenever asked about how the Saint Louis University Prison Program got started, I always explain that this is God's project. I have just made calls and knocked on doors. The first class began nine short months after that Sunday evening when I went to relax in front of *60 Minutes.*

The announcement of the program in the prison generated more than 300 applications in less than five days. Out of that pool we could select only fifteen students. They were an impressive group of men. Most had never attended college. Yet the students in our program had been GED tutors (preparing students for the high school equivalency diploma), facilitators in restorative justice groups, and several are autodidacts. One reads his New Testament in Greek. Another is an award-winning scriptwriter. There are self-taught musicians and artists. One student's academic skills are so advanced that he could easily pursue graduate studies. I discovered that there is great talent and extraordinary ability behind prison walls—human potential that we as a nation are wasting because we choose not to redirect and reshape that potential toward productive and positive purposes.

It must be emphasized that, as a Christian, it is not what I "do for prisoners" that has changed me. Students in prison have brought into my life the sacramental reality of Christ in the world in a new and transformative way. My colleague,

Grant Kaplan, has described his experience of teaching in prison this way:

> *"We normally use such words as 'volunteering' and 'service' when we describe our contact with those at the margins. But as good as these activities are, the vocabulary still indicates a distance between me and the other person… Instead I suggest that we [use the word] 'kinship.' Of course the experience of kinship is an experience of grace, and theology teaches us that grace is something that we do not earn, but is given to us. I do not know when it first happened, but I know when I first recognized it happening. It was Easter Friday [2010]…when we spent time talking about the length of the sentences being served. It was almost physically painful to imagine the time that so many [students] had left. And a semester of theology was such a small thing against the backdrop of 2019, or 2044, or life. Although it won't reduce [anyone's] sentence or make life inside easier, the truth is that the difference between student and teacher had been bridged in that classroom in a way unlike any previous classroom experience. I can only speak for myself in saying that I felt as though we truly belonged to one another. Paired with this insight was the question: If I can share this kinship with a class of felons, what prevents me from sharing the same kinship with my neighbors and the people who work in my building? So I've tried to keep this in my heart since Easter."*

Grant Kaplan observes that when people ask about his experience of teaching in prison:

"I'll tell them I learned here more than anywhere that we belong to one another, that the words of Jesus are indeed true, "that we may all be one, as you, Father, are in me and I in you, that they also may be in us" (John 17:21). Any division that separates me from my brothers and sisters comes from the sin in my own heart, and not from God's intended plan."

Raymond Scott, the valedictory speaker at our 2010 Bonne Terre prison graduation ceremony, described his education in the Saint Louis University Prison Program this way:

"In the Gospel of Matthew, chapter 25, verse 35, there is a passage that highlights my experience [of the program]. 'For I was hungry and you gave me food, I was thirsty and you gave me something to drink...' Personally, I was hungry for achievement, and thirsty for knowledge. Matthew 25 goes on to say, 'I was a stranger and you welcomed me, I was naked and you gave me clothing, I was sick and you took care of me.' Before [this program]...I was a stranger to myself, to my spiritual self—but not anymore. The professors helped me find my dignity again. I am no longer naked. Indeed they helped clothe me—not only with dignity, but with the sense of self-

worth that we all hunger and thirst for...The last passage from Matthew 25 reads, 'I was in prison and you came to visit me.' What you have done here for us—we who have long considered ourselves 'the least of these'—has had an incredible impact on us."

While Ray beautifully summarized his experience of the program through Scripture, my colleagues and I have discovered an even deeper truth in that passage. The "righteous" asked the king (Christ): *When had they welcomed him as a stranger, given him food and drink, clothed him, cared for him in illness, and visited him in prison?* The king responded, "Truly I tell you, just as you did it to one of the least of these who are members of my family, you did it to me." As professors have gone to the prison to teach, they have come back knowing that they have encountered Christ...and Christ came to them through persons who had committed murder, violence, sexual crimes, and more. We call the Saint Louis University Prison Program a Matthew 25 project, not because of what we "do for prisoners," but because we long to find Christ in our world.

This experience of the third element of belief in my life has made a mark on other faculty members, our students, and out into our community. My journey down this part of the Ethico-Mystical Way, has been the most exciting path of my life of faith yet. It has taught me how to turn my cries of despair—"What good can come of this?!"—into prayers of expectation, "Lord, what good can come of this? It is in your hands." It has been an extraordinary privilege to discover in places regarded as centers of hopelessness and despair the truth of Matthew 25. When I go to prison, I find Christ in my world!

Are there experiences in your journey of faith that have taken you to places you never expected to go? How have these emerged from your earlier experiences of the three elements of belief? How have experiences of *conversion of life* marked a new *way of life*? For your faith to grow and deepen, it is crucial that you be open to the third element of belief and be willing to allow it to transform you.

Yet never forget that the third element of belief alone cannot sustain you to the end of your journey. Living in the third element of belief, to the exclusion of the first and second elements, can lead to a distorted faith that draws you, and those who follow you, down a path of confusion and even destruction. We must now deal with that sad reality in the next chapter.

Meditation

As Christ is seen in the poor and in the persecuted, and in children, so is He seen in the employments which He puts upon His chosen whatever they be that in attending to his own calling he will be meeting Christ; that if he neglect it, he will not on that account enjoy His presence at all the more, but that while performing it, he will see Christ revealed to his soul amid the ordinary actions of the day, as by a sort of sacrament.

JOHN HENRY NEWMAN,
"DOING GLORY TO GOD IN PURSUIT OF THE WORLD,"
PAROCHIAL AND PLAIN SERMONS (1891, 8:165)

CHAPTER SIX

Dangers of the Adult's Way

In the previous chapter we explored the power of the third element of belief to transform lives and cultivate an interiorized faith. The Ethico-Mystical Way is that point beyond the external experiences of faith through the senses and authoritative voices of the first element of belief. The third element takes that step beyond our mind's ability to ask searching questions and find answers that satisfy our mind. Reason only gets us so far. At some point, committed action is required and we must trust that the mysteries of our faith will become clear in time. The Adult's Way draws on our affective, emotional selves and often involves breaking down our old lives in order for new life to be experienced.

We looked at *conversio morum* (conversion of life) as *conversatio morum* (way of life), the daily experience of living the Easter mystery of Christ's suffering, death, and resurrection. Rupture and crisis are often moments when the third element, the Ethico-Mystical Way, becomes the driving force in your life. This is the story of Saint Paul and Blessed John

Henry Newman. It has certainly been true in my experience of faith. I suspect that you have found it so in your spiritual journey as well. So we can see that this can be a great good and a means for the Spirit of God to redirect and remake lives that had not been bent toward the will of God.

Yet the third element of religion has its dark side as well. We must consider this and be conscious of its implications. Ronald Knox, a convert to Roman Catholicism and legendary Catholic chaplain at Oxford University during the mid-twentieth century, published a lengthy study on this subject in 1950. He titled his book *Enthusiasm* and used the term "suprasupernaturalism" to describe this excess. Knox traced this overemphasis on the third element of belief from earliest Christianity to his own time. As a historical theologian, I cringe at the way Knox tends to smooth out cultural and historical context to make his point...but I do acknowledge that he is on to something. Every generation of Christians has faced the challenge of suprasupernaturalism.

In Knox's reasoning, the root of this is a flawed understanding of grace. When best understood, grace is a perfection of nature, healing our brokenness and enabling us to function at a higher pitch—as Knox so eloquently put it—so that nature can play its part in the "music of eternity." Yet it always remains nature (Knox, 1950, 3).

Knox observed that the enthusiast is bolder and his understanding of grace is simpler. For the enthusiast, grace destroys nature and replaces it. The saved person is a new order of being with a different set of spiritual abilities in that transformed state. Direct inspiration from God is available at every turn if only the mind is abandoned, for that part of human nature was fatally damaged in the Garden of Eden (remember the use of reason in Genesis 3). While enthusiasts may conform outwardly to the powers of this world, they do not respect established authorities.

Here Knox pointed out flaws in suprasupernaturalism that are important to note: at its core enthusiasm is a rejection of both the first and second elements of belief. These have been left behind, for it is assumed that they are not needed in this transformed, superior state of being. It is an exaggerated notion of the third element of belief.

Knox observed that Paul dealt with some of these symptoms in the First Letter to the Corinthians, as he responded to issues raised by the Corinthians in their correspondence. For instance, Paul was troubled by the effort of some in Corinth to place a prohibition on sexual activity. Some in that church had declared, "It is well for a man not to touch a woman" (1 Corinthians 7:1). While Paul himself was celibate, he insisted that this was too harsh and would lead to immorality. He encouraged marriage and urged husbands and wives to express their love physically.

Knox also found that Tertullian, the great third-century North African theologian, indulged in suprasupernaturalism after a distinguished earlier career defending the faith. Tertullian's defense of the New Prophesy—what later became known as Montanism—eventually led to him being disciplined by the bishop of Rome. Three people who claimed to be prophets impressed him with claims of new revelations from the Holy Spirit. When criticized by bishops they separated from the Church, and Tertullian joined them. They claimed to be purer in their doctrine and more ascetical in their practice than other Christians. Their unwillingness to engage constructively with the church leaders or have their revelations analyzed and critically assessed by theologians represented an imbalance and rejection of the first and second elements of belief.

As Knox explored examples through the centuries, he highlighted the Donatists in later antiquity, the Albigenses and Waldenses in the Middle Ages, as well as the Anabaptists and Quakers during the early modern period. He singled out Methodism and the nineteenth-century revivalist movements that it inspired for particular criticism. In all of these cases, Knox reported a tendency to value a particular experience or expression of the faith and not place it into the broader context of the received structures of the faith (church, creeds, worship) and the rational explanations of Christian belief.

When I look more broadly at Christian history, other examples come to mind. One of the most striking examples of excessive dependence on the third element of belief can be found in a nineteenth-century movement in China. Because it is a story unfamiliar to most Western Christians, it offers a fresh example of harm that comes from claims to direct revelation from the Holy Spirit, disconnected from traditional Christian authority structures and rational critique.

This story begins with Hong Xiuquan, a mid-nineteenth-century Confucianist scholar who aspired to enter the Chinese civil service. The way to qualify was through a rigorous examination based on the Chinese classics. Though Hong was an accomplished scholar, he failed the test four times (only one percent of applicants ever passed these exams, and he was not rich enough to bribe the examiners). The strain of his efforts resulted in an emotional breakdown that disabled him for years. As he recovered he came under the influence of a Chinese Christian catechist from whom he received translations and summaries of the Christian Scriptures. Though he did not study them closely, they sparked his imagination. As he recovered in 1837, Hong had a series of what he took to be mystical visions. In one he was carried up to heaven and met a man who told him that China was full of demons and commanded Hong to purify his homeland. Hong identified this man as Jesus Christ, and he became convinced that he himself was Jesus' younger Chinese brother, who had been called to purify China and bring it to true faith. Hong preached this new gospel during the 1840s, and by 1850 he had gathered as many as 30,000 followers. Hong's version of Christianity gained influence, even as he became politically radical and violent. Through military force, by the end of the 1850s almost half of the Chinese empire fell under his control and he claimed the title of emperor for himself. The rise of the Heavenly Kingdom, also known as the Taiping Rebellion, is an example of the destructive power of the third element of belief, when that affective, mystical dimension of the religious experience crowds out and excludes the first and second elements of belief. Hong had no structures of authority to guide and limit his more extreme tendencies, and though he had mastered the Chinese classics, he had limited rational engagement with the Christian Scriptures and historic Christian teaching. This meant that he was reliant on his experience of faith. As he became more extreme, his actions and teachings became less and less connected from the message of Jesus in the gospels and millions died in his pursuit of the "Heavenly Kingdom."

Closer to our times and in this country, Jim Jones and his People's Temple comes to mind. This man, who had been a communist during the 1950s and a passionate desegregationist, also became a self-appointed pastor and taught his own version of the Christian faith. A charismatic preacher, Jones claimed direct inspiration from the Holy Spirit and drew a devoted following. He began to assert he was the reincarnation of Jesus of Nazareth, Mahatma Gandhi, the Buddha, and Vladimir Lenin. In the 1970s he led many hundreds to Guyana in South America and created Jonestown in the middle of a jungle. As he became more irrational, Jones demanded obedience to the visions he received from God. The situation became more ominous. I recall being in Berkeley visiting friends for Thanksgiving when the Jonestown Massacre occurred. More than 900 men, women, and children died in a mass suicide that Jim Jones had been preparing for some time. Over the years I have met family and friends of his followers who still struggle to make sense of the deaths of loved ones. This is another tragic example of suprasupernaturalism taken to extremes.

You are not likely to come into contact with such strange and radical forms of suprasupernaturalism found in Hong Xiuquan or Jim Jones. However, there will be occasions when you encounter persons whose spiritual teaching and example may tempt you "to move beyond" or abandon the first and second elements of belief in the quest for their higher spiritual state. I have never lived in any locality where instances of this have not been present. Whenever a priest, mentor, or spiritual leader encourages you to do just that...beware!

This dark side of the third element belief is the result of a failure to harmonize the Ethico-Mystical Way with the other two elements. When the other elements are neglected, the results are often distortions and exaggerations in belief and practice. As has been noted, an unbalanced third element of belief can be the most dangerous of the three. One can be deceived into pursuing destructive actions in the absence of the traditional, historic, and external dimension of belief, or the reasoning and questioning aspect of faith.

While I have focused much of this chapter on large movements through history and leaders who have been prone to dramatic excesses, we also encounter damaging dependence on the third element in the lives of people around us. This overdependence on direct inspiration and an emotional response can result in a shallow spirituality. This was the struggle I had growing up in the Holiness tradition. It became clearer as I grew that there was an unhealthy dependence on my affective experience of faith. This premature focus on my interior response to the call of faith left me feeling rootless and disconnected from Christians in the past as well as in the present. My conception of Christian faith seemed disengaged from my intellectual quest to understand Christian doctrines, and my desire to appreciate what Christians shared in common, as well as what distinguished them doctrinally. This caused me to fear that my questioning meant that I was losing my Christian faith.

Yet as we noted earlier, the challenge of an unbalanced faith is not limited to an overemphasis on the third element of belief. This is true for the other two elements as well. Any stress on one element of belief over the other two can lead to stunted growth in the lives of believers and in the ethos of Christian communities. Balance is what is needed.

This is a wonderful ideal, but can it be achieved? When you look at yourself and your Christian community, do you find balance between the three elements? Because this is not a static experience, it is always a work in progress. I would be surprised if you found a perfect balance between the three elements. But the goal is not perfection, but rather a growing awareness of how the three elements function in your experience of Christian belief, as well as in the faith life of others. By recognizing these elements as authentic expressions of faith, it opens the way to greater patience with yourself and deeper compassion for others who may—in the midst of their own imperfection—be striving for the harmony that you seek as well. In short, understanding how the three elements function can promote charity and compassion, a message central to Jesus' teachings in the gospels.

In the concluding chapter we will consider how these elements, when functioning together, can promote a "grown-up" faith that blends these seemingly conflicting parts of yourself, brings you into a greater understanding of yourself, and cultivates in you a deeper love and compassion for others. Because this synergy is best understood in concrete experience rather than abstract description, the life of John Henry Newman will be used as a model to analyze and an example to follow.

Meditation

I believe because I am told, because it is true, because it answers to my deepest interior experiences and needs. And, everything else being equal, my faith will be at its richest and deepest and strongest, in so far as all three motives are most fully and characteristically operative within me, at one and the same time, and towards one and the same ultimate result and end.

FRIEDRICH VON HÜGEL,
MYSTICAL ELEMENT OF RELIGION (1909), 54.

SECTION IV

Concluding Remarks

Chapter Seven

The Synergy of the Three Elements of Belief

Blessed are they who give the flower of their days and their strength of soul and body to Him; blessed are they who in their youth turn to Him, who gave His life for them and would fain give it to them and implant it in them that they may live for ever. Blessed are they who resolve—come good, come evil, come sunshine, come tempest, come honor, come dishonor—that He shall be their Lord and Master, their King and God! They will come to a perfect end and to peace at the last.

JOHN HENRY NEWMAN
PAROCHIAL AND PLAIN SERMONS (1868), 8:243

Throughout this book, the experience of John Henry Newman has been used to exemplify how the three elements of belief function in the life of a Christian, and can be manifested in the corporate life of the Church—what Saint Paul called "Christ's Body." Newman was honored late in his own lifetime by Pope Leo XIII, who elevated him to be a cardinal in 1879 for his work as a Catholic theologian. We have already noted that Pope Paul VI associated the questions he raised with important documents proclaimed by the Second Vatican Council. In 1991, Pope John Paul II gave Newman the title "Venerable," which is reserved for individuals who are deemed to have lived a life of "heroic virtue." In 2010, Pope Benedict XVI beatified Newman, which is the final step before being declared a saint by the Catholic Church.

If you just look at these honors bestowed by popes, it would be easy to imagine that you have nothing in common with John Henry Newman. He must have lived in a manner that is beyond that of any "ordinary" Christian. Yet we have found that he struggled with human challenges that we all recognize. The same is true of the Church of his generation. His life of faith—and the experience of being a devoted member of the Catholic Church—was not simple or easy.

The religious imagination that he received in childhood did not form him to live the Christian faith as a Catholic. In fact, the authorities of his early life assured him that Roman Catholicism was a corrupt and distorted expression of Christianity. He spent his first twenty years as a scholar and theologian gathering evidence and arguments to convince others that the Anglican faith he had received as a child was *the path* to salvation. It was not until age forty-five that he became convinced that despite all of his arguments and protests to the contrary, he must become a Roman Catholic. He spent the rest of his ninety years on a journey to understand his Christian faith in the context of the Catholic Church.

It would be a mistake to assume that he lived as a Catholic in passive obedience to Church authorities, or that he received widespread acclaim and approval from Church officials for his brilliant work as a theologian—far from it. Some Catholic leaders during his lifetime did not regard him as a venerable example of "heroic virtue," and certainly not a candidate for sainthood. His forty-five years as a Catholic were marked by long periods of turmoil and suspicion that his writings were not orthodox. In the years just after he became a Catholic, some Church leaders regarded his theory of doctrinal development (that Christian truth emerges in its fullness over time in human history) as heretical. Yet the Second Vatican Council incorporated his concept of development into its documents, and Pope Benedict XVI has described it as central to a Catholic understanding of how Christian truth comes to us. The great Dominican theologian, Marie-Dominique Chenu, who was so influential at Vatican II, indicated that truth is not lessened for being etched in time. This insight came into the Catholic Church through the personal intellectual struggle of the Protestant theologian, John Henry

Newman, in the last stages of his discernment to become a Roman Catholic. As the "Body of Christ," we have grown in the second element of belief because of his insight.

When Newman published an article titled "On Consulting the Faithful in Matters of Doctrine"—an optimistic estimation of the work of the Holy Spirit in the collective experience of the people of God—one Vatican official described Newman as the most dangerous man in England and spoke disparagingly of lay Catholics. His own bishop asked him with a disbelieving tone, "Who *are* the laity?" Newman observed that the Church would look rather foolish without them. For more than a decade after that he lived under a cloud of pending judgment from Rome. When I look back on this, I wonder whether those leaders were struggling with some of the difficulties and challenges of the first element of belief.

Yet the bishops at Vatican II, inspired by Newman's optimism, explained in its texts the vital role of the laity in the life of the Church. Had Newman lived his faith exclusively in the first element of belief, he might have been crushed by this disapproval and silenced by these powerful people. Yet he never lost faith that, over time, the Holy Spirit achieved God's best through the leadership structures of the Catholic Church. The writings for which he had been most vilified in his own time became the cornerstones of his reputation and the grounds for acclaim by twentieth- and twenty-first-century popes.

Newman's experience with the second element of belief

was dynamic and vigorous. This rational, inquiring aspect of faith gave life and vitality to his work as a theologian. It also caused him much suffering. At times he questioned the prudence and wisdom of decisions being made by some Church authorities. Lord John Acton described one such occasion, when in a three-hour conversation Newman stood by the fireplace rocking back and forth like a person with a toothache. He lamented the natural tendency of powerful men to tyrannize, and deplored the ignorance and presumption of some who imagined themselves to be competent theologians. He understood the fallibility of Church leaders, and their capacity to be motivated by prejudice, limited understanding, and desire for promotion. He knew enough about the history of Christianity to be aware that his age was no different. Church leaders are not immune from the difficulties and challenges of the first element of belief. Yet his experience of the third element of belief enabled him to rest confident that God's work is accomplished in *God's* timing and not dependent on him. His task was to be faithful to the work God had placed before him.

Newman sought to live in obedience to Church teaching and the authorities in his life as a priest. Yet he raised uncomfortable questions when necessary and paid dearly for his thoughtful and incisive analysis of challenges facing the Catholic Church in his day. However, he also learned how to let go and trust God's presence in the world and in the life of the Church. The third element of belief carried him through these tough times, beyond controversies that filled others with despair. Yet how did he do this in his lived experience?

Perhaps the best example of this was the way Newman engaged the debates over defining papal infallibility in the 1860s and at the First Vatican Council in 1870. While he believed that in certain circumstances popes could infallibly settle doctrinal questions, he was emphatic in private correspondence and conversation that the Church had not reached a clear consensus on this subject. Newman did not believe the 1860s were the right time to define papal infallibility. In fact, he feared that an extreme theological opinion was being foisted on the Church by what he called an "aggressive and insolent faction." During the First Vatican Council Newman complained to his bishop and asked why Catholics were being forced to deal with a matter that was not a pressing necessity. When another bishop wrote and explained that his theory of doctrinal development was being used to defend the plan to define papal infallibility, Newman expressed exasperation. He observed that for years he had been criticized for his writings on development, and now this concept was being used in favor of a cause he did not support. But in a fascinating moment of self-reflection, he noted that he did not regret it, because he would not have become a Catholic without having thought through the theory of doctrinal development during his last years as a Protestant.

When papal infallibility was defined by the council, Newman accepted it and expressed relief that the extreme faction had not gotten all that they had wanted. In fact, the definition was very narrow. We still only have two clear instances when papal infallibility has been invoked in the history of the Catholic Church, according to Vatican I's explanation of that doctrine.

But Newman had friends and disciples who were convinced that this would be the end of the Church. To one of these, he urged patience. He recalled the example of earlier councils and noted that full truth had never been achieved at a single council. Often multiple councils, making decisions in different directions, were needed before a settled understanding was achieved. This sometimes took hundreds of years. Newman observed that Pius IX would not be the last pope and Vatican I would not be the last council. He urged his friends to have faith in the Holy Spirit at work in the Church and expressed confidence that in time a new pope and a new council would achieve greater balance. As it turned out, he was right. But it did not happen in his lifetime. "Newman's hour" came almost a century later.

You may be wondering what all of this has to do with your quest for a "grown-up" faith and how it applies to your efforts to blend the three elements of belief. After all, you are not looking to lead the Church but to live out the Christian life in its fullness where you are.

Newman was no different, and he longed for the same thing. In one of his sermons, Newman expressed it this way:

"We shall find it difficult to estimate the moral power which a single individual, trained to practice what he teaches, may acquire in his own circle, in the course of years" ("On Personal Influence," *University Sermons*, 94). Newman did not set out to change the Church. He sought to change himself—to experience *conversion of life* as a *way of life*. Instead of going to Rome to be an influential theologian at the First Vatican Council (three bishops and the pope asked him to come!), Newman respectfully declined and stayed in Birmingham, England, to finish thinking through and writing about what it means to submit to Christian truth. His *Grammar of Assent*, a study of how Christians come to believe, remains one of his greatest works. It is a study that articulates in a profound and sophisticated way the three elements of belief that have been explored in this book. By seeking to be faithful to his personal quest for a "grown-up" faith in difficult times, he not only changed himself and the small circle around him. Newman's faithfulness to blending the three elements of belief changed the Church he loved—generations after his death.

Newman exemplifies for me the importance of living an intentional, reflective Christian faith. Like him, I recognize the necessity of living within the context of a received Christian tradition to which I am accountable while never forgetting that God has given me a mind that seeks understanding. Yet Newman's life is a constant reminder that despite my best effort to understand, there are things that I must leave in God's hands, in trusting hope that over time God's best will be achieved. It is not my role to change the world but to be a catalyst for change if that is God's intention.

I began studying Newman's life while doing post-doctoral studies at the University of Fribourg in Switzerland in the late 1980s. At that time I was a Benedictine monk living with Dominican professors and students at the Albertinum. It was an exciting place to live, because some of the professors were trusted advisors to Pope John Paul II and leading figures in the Vatican. It was not uncommon for these scholars to leave in the middle of a meal to take a call from Joseph Cardinal Ratzinger (now Pope Benedict XVI) or other top-ranking leaders in the Curia. The *Catechism of the Catholic Church* was being edited by one of these men, and I had the privilege of helping with translation work on some of the early drafts.

Fribourg was an exciting place because the breadth and diversity of the Roman Catholic experience was evident all around me. One professor in that community taught at Archbishop Marcel Lefebvre's traditionalist seminary (until his Society of Saint Pius X broke completely with the Catholic Church). Another wrote on liberation theology and sought to integrate Marxist dialectics into his theology. There were biblical scholars who did impressive historical critical analysis of Scripture and theologians who sought to revive in a modern setting the medieval scholastic tradition. One professor had substantially written one of John Paul II's most important and controversial encyclicals. So much seemed to be in turmoil. The powerful personalities and ambitions of certain men made a deep impression on me.

Studying Newman's life and example helped me realize there has never been a time when the Church has lived in settled times. He once observed, "in each age, as it comes, we shall read of tumult and heresy, and hear the complaint of good men marvelling at what they conceive to be the especial wickedness of their own times" ("On Personal Influence," *University Sermons*, 84). Every generation must face the complex challenge of respectful obedience to Church authorities while not shying away from the pressing questions and issues of the times. Living so closely with people who were helping make decisions that had an impact on the whole Church made me aware of the humanity of our leaders. They struggle with the promise and challenge of blending the three elements of belief like the rest of us. But it also made me conscious of their deep desire to be attuned to the guidance of the Holy Spirit. It was a time when I learned to feel compassion for those called to bear the burden of leadership. In my own way, I began to try and follow Newman's example of blending the three elements of belief.

This meant respectfully engaging Church teaching and the guidance of Church leaders while not abandoning questions that I had. Following Newman's example, I learned not to shy away from the hard task of thinking through knotty issues and seeking as much knowledge as possible to understand them in their complexity. Yet Newman also inspired me to recognize that at times I must let go of my own understanding and trust that God will direct my path and find a way forward for the Church (Proverbs 3:5–6).

This is not simple. In fact it is often a messy process. But Newman's concept of development has helped me keep things in perspective and not despair when I have found myself disagreeing with a position taken on one subject or another by Church leaders or other Catholics. As long as debates and differences in the Church are conducted in a manner that reflects Christian charity and Christ's summary of the law—to love God with all your being and your neighbor as yourself—I do not fear these tensions. But even when they do not exemplify Christ's law of love, I strive to live in trust and hope that God's best will prevail. It may not be in my lifetime. Yet it is not my task to "solve" these problems but to witness to the truth that I have come to understand.

While Newman was not loved and admired by some of the most powerful men in Rome, it is now his teaching and example that we are urged to follow by Pope Benedict XVI and others. Men who exercised far greater influence and power than Newman in the 1800s are now all but forgotten. Newman's faithfulness to his journey of faith made all the difference and set him on a path that has inspired others to follow. One of the great ironies of his legacy is that he is loved by the broad spectrum of Catholics in our day. For conservative Catholics, he is the great champion of tradition and obedience to hierarchical authority as well as a witness to the compelling historical continuity of the Roman Catholic Church with earliest Christianity. For progressive Catholics, Newman embodies what it means to think, inquire, and ponder the possibility that the Holy Spirit is moving the people of God to address pressing issues of our times. For all Christians, he models what it means to step beyond what we have been told and what we can understand and—trusting God—walk down a path that may take us to places we never imagined we would go. Newman expressed this best in one of his famous hymns, "The Pillar of the Cloud":

> Lead, Kindly Light, amid the encircling gloom
> Lead Thou me on!
> The night is dark, and I am far from home—
> Lead Thou me on!
> Keep Thou my feet; I do not ask to see
> The distant scene—one step enough for me.

Newman's life of faith had all of these elements blended together. Because of the synergy of their interaction, he not only lived a life of "heroic virtue" but remains a model—not of *perfection*—but of *perseverance*. No doubt he will soon be declared a saint. But I hope we never forget that his was a long and complicated journey of faith—much like yours and mine.

In your quest for a full and mature faith, always remember that you cannot live in just one of the elements of belief or try to leave one or more of them behind. You must live in the challenging, dynamic experience of blending the three. Like Newman, you will never achieve perfection. Yet by seeking to live your faith to its fullest, you will discover new ways that Christ will be present to you and learn what it means for others to find Christ in you. Be willing to submit in humble obedience when necessary, respect your questions and seek answers as best you can, and be willing to step out in trust when life's challenges open new paths to discover God in your world. If you do, your spiritual journey will not only change you but all who are touched by your life of faith.

Meditation

[People] commonly held in popular estimation are greatest at a distance; they become small as they are approached; but the attraction, exerted by unconscious holiness, is of an urgent and irresistible nature; it persuades the weak, the timid, the wavering, and the inquiring; it draws forth the affection and loyalty of all who are in a measure like-minded; and over the thoughtless or perverse multitude it exercises a sovereign compulsory sway, bidding them fear and keep silence, on the ground of its own divine [right] to rule them,—its hereditary claim on their obedience, though they understand not the principles or counsels of that spirit, which is "born, not of blood, nor of the will of the flesh, nor of the will of man, but of God" (Newman, "On Personal Influence," *University Sermons*, 95).

Meditations on the Life of Faith

BY JOHN HENRY NEWMAN

God has created all things for good; all things for their greatest good; everything for its own good. What is the good of one is not the good of another; what makes one man happy would make another unhappy. God has determined, unless I interfere with His plan, that I should reach that which will be my greatest happiness. He looks on me individually, He calls me by my name, He knows what I can do, what I can best be, what is my greatest happiness, and He means to give it me.

God knows what is my greatest happiness, but I do not. There is no rule about what is happy and good; what suits one would not suit another. And the ways by which perfection is reached vary very much; the medicines necessary for our souls are very different from each other. Thus God leads us by strange ways; we know He wills our happiness, but we neither know what our happiness is, nor the way. We are blind; left to ourselves we should take the wrong way; we must leave it to Him.

Let us put ourselves into His hands, and not be startled though He leads us by a strange way, a mirabilis via [wonderful/glorious/miraculous way], as the Church speaks. Let us be sure He will lead us right, that He will bring us to that which is, not indeed what we think best, nor what is best for another, but what is best for us.

Prayer

O, my God, I will put myself without reserve into Thy hands. Wealth or woe, joy or sorrow, friends or bereavement, honour or humiliation, good report or ill report, comfort or discomfort, Thy presence or the hiding of Thy countenance, all is good if it comes from Thee. Thou art wisdom and Thou art love—what can I desire more? Thou hast led me in Thy counsel, and with glory hast Thou received me. What have I in heaven, and apart from Thee what want I upon earth? My flesh and my heart faileth: but God is the God of my heart, and my portion for ever.

MARCH 6, 1848
MEDITATIONS AND DEVOTIONS OF THE LATE CARDINAL NEWMAN (1907), 299–300

God was all-complete, all-blessed in Himself; but it was His will to create a world for His glory. He is Almighty, and might have done all things Himself, but it has been His will to bring about His purposes by the beings He has created. We are all created to His glory—we are created to do His will. I am created to do something or to be something for which no one else is created; I have a place in God's counsels, in God's world, which no one else has; whether I be rich or poor, despised or esteemed by man, God knows me and calls me by my name.

God has created me to do Him some definite service; He has committed some work to me which He has not committed to another. I have my mission—I never may know it in this life, but I shall be told it in the next. Somehow I am necessary for His purposes, as necessary in my place as an Archangel in his—if, indeed, I fail, He can raise another, as He could make the stones children of Abraham. Yet I have a part in this great work; I am a link in a chain, a bond of connexion between persons. He has not created me for naught. I shall do good, I shall do His work; I shall be an angel of peace, a preacher of truth in my own place, while not intending it, if I do but keep His commandments and serve Him in my calling.

Therefore I will trust Him. Whatever, wherever I am, I can never be thrown away. If I am in sickness, my sickness may serve Him; in perplexity, my perplexity may serve Him; if I am in sorrow, my sorrow may serve Him. My sickness, or perplexity, or sorrow may be necessary causes of some great end, which is quite beyond us. He does nothing in vain; He may prolong my life, He may shorten it; He knows what He is about. He may take away my friends, He may throw me among strangers, He may make me feel desolate, make my spirits sink, hide the future from me—still He knows what He is about.

Prayer

O *Adonai*, O Ruler of Israel, Thou that guidest Joseph like a flock, O Emmanuel, O Sapientia, I give myself to Thee. I trust Thee wholly. Thou art wiser than I—more loving to me than I myself. Deign to fulfill Thy high purposes in me whatever they be—work in and through me. I am born to serve Thee, to be Thine, to be Thy instrument. Let me be Thy blind instrument. I ask not to see—I ask not to know—I ask simply to be used.

MARCH 7, 1848
MEDITATIONS AND DEVOTIONS OF THE LATE CARDINAL NEWMAN (1907), 300–302

What mind of man can imagine the love which the Eternal Father bears towards the Only Begotten Son? It has been from everlasting,—and it is infinite; so great is it that divines call the Holy Ghost by the name of that love, as if to express its infinitude and perfection. Yet reflect, O my soul, and bow down before the awful mystery, that, as the Father loves the Son, so doth the Son love thee, if thou art one of His elect; for He says expressly, "As the Father hath loved Me, I also have loved you. Abide in My love." What mystery in the whole circle of revealed truths is greater than this? The love which the Son bears to thee, a creature, is like that which the Father bears to the uncreated Son. O wonderful mystery! This, then, is the history of what else is so strange: that He should have taken my flesh and died for me. The former mystery anticipates the latter; that latter does but fulfill the former. Did He not love me so inexpressibly, He would not have suffered for me. I understand now why He died for me, because He loved me as a father loves his son—not as a human father merely, but as the Eternal Father the Eternal Son. I see now the meaning of that else inexplicable humiliation: He preferred to regain me rather than to create new worlds.

How constant is He in His affection! He has loved us from the time of Adam. He has said from the beginning, "I will never leave thee nor forsake thee." He did not forsake us in our sin. He did not forsake me. He found me out and regained me. He made a point of it—He resolved to restore me, in spite of myself, to that blessedness which I was so obstinately set against. And now what does He ask of me, but that, as He has loved me with an everlasting love, so I should love Him in such poor measures as I can show.

Prayer

O mystery of mysteries, that the ineffable love of Father to Son should be the love of the Son to us! Why was it, O Lord? What good thing didst Thou see in me a sinner? Why wast Thou set on me? "What is man, that Thou art mindful of him, and the son of man that Thou visitest him?" This poor flesh of mine, this weak sinful soul, which has no life except in Thy grace, Thou didst set Thy love upon it. Complete Thy work, O Lord, and as Thou hast loved me from the beginning, so make me to love Thee unto the end.

MARCH 7, 1848
MEDITATIONS AND DEVOTIONS OF THE LATE CARDINAL NEWMAN (1907), 302–304